THE EXMOOR FILES

THE EXMOOR FILES

*   *   *

*How I Lost a Husband
and Found Rural Bliss*

Liz Jones

Weidenfeld & Nicolson

LONDON

First published in Great Britain in 2009
by Weidenfeld & Nicolson

1 3 5 7 9 10 8 6 4 2

A CIP catalogue record for this book
is available from the British Library.

ISBN- 978 0297 85443 2

Typeset by Input Data Services Ltd,
Bridgwater, Somerset

Printed and bound in the UK by
CPI Mackays, Chatham ME5 8TD

The Orion Publishing Group's policy is to use papers
that are natural, renewable and recyclable products and
made from wood grown in sustainable forests. The logging
and manufacturing processes are expected to conform to
the environmental regulations of the country of origin.

Weidenfeld & Nicolson

The Orion Publishing Group Ltd
Orion House
5 Upper Saint Martin's Lane,
London, WC2H 9EA

An Hachette UK Company

www.orionbooks.co.uk

For Lizzie
and Snoopy

'All alone, all by myself
Growing old and quite on the shelf.'

Dodie Smith

CAST OF CHARACTERS

* * *

Me. Liz or Lizzie. I like to flatter myself by believing I bear a passing resemblance to Lizzie Bennet: shunned by men, bright but not beautiful, likes to sit in a corner reading by flickering candlelight (mine are scented; hers probably weren't), no central heating, forced into long country walks in inclement weather, the bottoms of clothes always stained by mud. Bit of a cross patch. As well as Lizzie Bennet, the fictional person in history I resemble most is Tess of the D'Urbervilles: I can often be found in the dead of night, feeling thwarted and hard done by, digging up turnips from the frosty earth, wailing (bleating) that whatever youthful allure I possessed is now hopelessly wasted, lashed as it is by hailstones and wind. A former editor of a fashion magazine, lifelong slave to sartorial swings and roundabouts (I once bought two pairs of identical buttery suede Pocahontas trousers from Alberta Ferretti, just in case one developed a smudge), living proof that 30 years of waxing your legs does not make the hairs grow back scarcer and finer. Destined, hopefully, for a happy ending or if not a reasonably early, 18th-century death. As Charlotte so aptly put it in *Sex and the City*: 'I've been dating since I was 15. I'm exhausted! Where *is* he!!' Honestly, single women were not meant to live beyond the age of 41.

Lizzie. Another Lizzie, this time a seven-year-old former racehorse with a nervous disposition and tendency to lash out. A 15 hands 3 inches dappled, bright bay in summer, a darker chocolate brown in winter, with a mealy mouth that makes her closely resemble Homer Simpson. A couple of white hairs in the middle of her forehead that are a sorry excuse for a star. A round, stress-fat tummy (a bit like her mummy's). A tail that is so thin and wispy I honestly think she needs extensions (unlike my hair which my ex-husband – of whom not *too* much more later – thought so thick and coarse it surely belonged on an equine). A tendency to be a little bit of a fidget. Prone to princess-dom. I sometimes preface her name with the word 'Violet'.

Benji. A 12–year-old New Forest pony with a bolshy disposition, enormous brown, liquid eyes framed by dark eyeliner and a huge bottom. Benji had 12 owners before he came to me a week before he was due to be shot. Horrible children had probably kicked him in his ribs and then abandoned him to a muddy field once they discovered X Boxes/the opposite sex/illegal substances. Loves eating; confused by peanut butter.

Dream. Ah, Dream. I love Dream. Another New Forest pony who is so small, tiny (about 11 hands), but with enormous character. She has a wide blaze, big eyes, a bouffant and, to be honest, very Eighties mane, and lips that can magically stretch across the yard to steal carrots from your pockets. A tendency to turn her bottom on you and let loose with both barrels. She broke her pelvis early in life, which means she now moves like a crab; she frequently misses a corner and disappears into the distance until she can at last turn round, her big eyes wide with anxiety in case she has missed something, anything.

Maggie. A former event horse who became, in the words of her owner, 'dangerous and naughty' when out competing. Like Benji, she was also days away from being taken to slaughter. Honestly, it's a blood bath out here in the countryside, like the first 20 minutes of *Saving Private Ryan*. I soon found out that, rather than being naughty, Maggie has a bad back, a misplaced pelvis, one front hoof smaller than the rest, an abscess brewing in said hoof, and chronic agoraphobia: if you let her off in a field, she drops to the ground in a frantic roll, scrambles to her feet, then takes off at full pelt, ending up in a corner where she will just stand, looking worried. But in the orchard, which is small and which she can share with the three lambs (see below), she is absolutely fine. As Sybil Fawlty said of her mother, 'It's quite hard getting the space right, really.' A very dark bay with a tiny white star, she's less compact than Lizzie, far more rangy at 16 hands 2 inches, and 12 years old. She has a beautiful face and when stood in the stable her lower lip droops, so she most closely resembles Zippy from *Rainbow*.

Michael. Also known as Badger, because he looks like one, or 'fleabag', because he keeps scratching with a smile on his face, and is generally referred to as 'my new boy-friend'. Michael is a sheepdog who, unfortunately, if he ever gets near a sheep tries to remove its entrails, which is probably why he was abandoned, filthy and starving, by the side of a B road in the middle of an Exmoor winter. His teeth are tiny stumps, which means he either spent most of his life on the end of a chain, trying to gnaw himself free, or his owner was trying to stop him removing the entrails from sheep. He stands in a very hangdog, Gromit-like stance when he can't have his own way. When he rolls on the hideous carpet he makes a sound like Spotty Dog from the Woodentops. He gets very stiff in the evenings; he really should take a leaf out of the cats' book and do more yoga. Very good with the cats (of whom *much* more later). Not quite so good with the chickens: he tries to herd them against their will and with much clucking – on the chickens' part – into the corner of a stable. Was very well-behaved when I first got him – he would actually cower when I went to put on his lead – but very soon started climbing all over me to steal my morning chocolate digestive. Hates wheelbarrows, the rain and the smart navy coat that makes him the laughing stock of all the other sheepdogs in the vicinity – hard, barky things that live outside and never have their paws washed.

The chickens. This is a group entry for Veronica, Gwen and Cokey. Former battery hens (I'm convinced they have flashbacks and suffer from post-traumatic stress disorder), they now live in the orchard (this sounds more picturesque than it actually is: more a patch of feral grass with a few wizened trees that have obviously gone through the menopause, apple-wise) with a wooden house for a bedroom, Le Creuset dishes for their organic grain and vegetable peelings. They are under *absolutely no pressure at all* to actually produce an egg. Whenever they spot me on the horizon they gallop towards me like crazy, tiny ostriches.

The lambs. These sweet little creatures – Caitlin, who has straight horns and a dark face; Ash, who's quite big, almost reaching past my Hunter wellies; and Willow, who's so desperately shy she reminds me of myself at a mid-Seventies disco (even now, if I hear the strains of the Stylistics' 'Betcha by Golly Wow', I become extremely nervous) – most closely resemble clouds on sticks. They are Shetlands, which means they're quite rare (almost as rare as giant pandas and Exmoor ponies), have very thick, almost Rastafarian coats that frequently become entangled in hawthorn, resulting in lots of plaintive bleating (on my part. Last night, my left hand would not stop tingling and I immediately thought, oh dear God, I have multiple sclerosis, and then I remembered I had plunged said hand into a bed of nettles, armed with secateurs, to snip Willow free from thorns). When it rains, as it does every day, without fail, here in deepest Somerset, they smell like wet jumpers.

The fur babies. Ahhhh. My babies. Even though I didn't squeeze these little creatures from between my over-aerobicised thighs (once by expensive, twice-weekly Pilates lessons; now by pushing wheelbarrows through rutted mud), I couldn't possibly love them any more than

I do. To recap for anyone unfamiliar with these plump, wilful, spoilt beings:

- Snoopy is the original cat, a tabby with white paws, a white bib and a liking for kisses on the top of his head; he loves pasta.
- Squeaky is the matriarch of the pack, a black puss (a Bombay, to be precise) with the dense fur of a mole and round yellow eyes; she has been known, due to her considerable girth, to wear the cat flap as a skirt. When she lies down, she makes the shape of a hovercraft.
- Susie, a former feral kitten, is as sleek as an otter, as beautiful as a leopard and as slender and difficult as a supermodel. Sleeps each night in the crook of my arm or around my neck and gives me a really hard stare if I sneeze. Now that she has barns and log piles to patrol, she has a permanently thrilled face.
- Sweetie, middle name 'Biscuit': clumsy, stripy, with great big furry trousers. If you pick her up, she barks like a dog. Has learned to lick me in my mouth (yes, that was 'in' not 'on'). Since moving to the countryside has found she loves galloping across the fields like a horse, climbing trees as long as she can get up a good spurt first, and teasing the chickens. Hates being dive-bombed by swallows: you can actually see her going, as she ducks and looks over her shoulder, 'Just bugger off. I'm not going to climb into your muddy, spittled nest; I'm more interested in catching voles and placing them on Mummy's pillow.'

Brian (Brain). The gardener. Comes two days a week to push leaves around. Has such a pronounced West Country accent I've no idea what he is talking about; I just stare at him blankly. A little bit defeatist, always telling me I can't do things: 'Ooh no, you don't want to do thaaaaa't.' Helps me to split logs. Manages the vegetable patch. Honestly, after buying all the tiny plants, 'muck' (I have my own muck, courtesy of the horses, but this was deemed 'not the right sort'; in a similar vein, I was told by Patrick the sheepfarmer, who has the rather untidy farm along from me, that the grass in my fields is 'not suitable for hay', which means I have to purchase it instead), the wooden posts, the topsoil, the chicken wire needed to keep the rabbits out (I wasn't really averse to letting them in) and on and on and on, it would've been far cheaper to have had an organic vegetable box flown to my house once a week by Abel and Cole in London. Brian laughed when the carefully nurtured (by me) wildflower meadow reaped precisely three varieties of rare, ancient English flora: pre-historic, Journey-to-the-Centre-of-the-Earth-size dock leaves, shepherd's purse (scant) and nettles (lots).

The ex-husband. Hmmmm. What can I say? Married for four years (to me). Nightmare honeymoon. Twenty-six when I met him (he was 26. I wasn't. I was, in fact, 14 years older than him, depending on the time of year. My age involved me in lots of *Tess of the D'Urbervilles*-style lying, which meant, like her, I was rather unfairly punished and abandoned; I fully expect to be hung at some point). The ex-husband now lives in Delhi, which means he isn't really 'lost', as mentioned in the title to this book, more at extreme arm's length, where I'm hoping he has run to fat and premature male pattern baldness. Prone to laziness and rampant infidelity. I knew our marriage was destined to fail when, one afternoon, I stumbled upon him in our basement kitchen doing an impression of me for his best friend (this friend would also be his best man, but they fell out when my husband based a character in his 'novel' on him). My husband was using the bottom of his T-shirt in an OCD fashion to open the stainless-steel Sub-Zero fridge, wailing in a high-pitched voice, 'I need my space! I need my space!' The reason I moved to live in the middle of bloody Exmoor in the bleeding first place. Quite useful for blaming for absolutely everything that has ever happened to me, from the moment I was born until such time as I am lain (oh happy release) beneath a yellow lichen-covered (the air is delightfully clean here) headstone that reads: 'Here lies Miss Jones. Barren pet lover whose last wish was to please, please, please not chisel on here the date she was born. Found it very hard to get warm/ dates/the horses in.'

Emily. A goddess. A beautiful, curvaceous young lady who runs the local delicatessen, the only institution that separates me from foraging in frozen hedgerows and, ultimately, starvation. So posh she calls her parents 'Mother and Father'. Wears sparkly eyeshadow, pale lipstick that gives her a ghostly air, an apron, elaborate knitwear and roars around the lanes in a brand new Mercedes sports car. Her boyfriend lives in my village. They are the only people under 30 within a radius of 200 miles.

Nicola. Helps me to look after my horses, being an expert in equine touch (a non-invasive form of massage), flow (an even gentler form of massage), aromatherapy,

Bach flower remedies, Reiki, nutrition, use of herbs and magic poultices. She likes to put a completely silent CD on the machine in the tack room for healing purposes. Has a dog she found at the roadside with a broken leg, covered in cigarette burns, and a serene, Buddhist boyfriend. A wonderful woman with an East End accent and propensity for punching people who hunt deer or shoot pheasants and grouse on Exmoor full in the face. I used to think the signs on the roads on the moor saying, 'Slow, pheasants', were kind, not realising they just wanted to preserve the poor birds for the gun sights. When Lizzie, in a very good impression of a velociraptor, swings her neck to bite her, Nic shrugs her shoulders and says, 'Am I bovvered though?' When we are out riding (I say that so nonchalantly, don't I, when it took a year to even sit on my horse), she will spot a man driving a tractor and say, 'He's well crumpet. Proper farmer crumpet!' Has a huge, handsome grey horse called Quincy, with enormous hooves, who is now Lizzie's husband. They are inseparable. Lizzie is often to be found resting her chin in the soft hammock of Quincy's broad back, Penélope Cruzworthy eyelashes fluttering, 'He adores me, I deserve it. What more is there to life than this?' Not the fate, unfortunately, of her human namesake.

The moor. It surrounds me, sometimes like a buffer against the modern world, at other times like a cloud, or a necklace that is about to suffocate me. The moor has moods, would you believe it, and can be very dangerous: you don't ever want to get lost or run out of petrol on the moor (of the few petrol stations still in existence, most close early every day, and don't even open at weekends, giving the moor a faintly Amish air). More beautiful, I think, than nearby Dartmoor, which has a prison, more roads and a bleaker atmosphere. I don't think I will ever get to know every inch of Exmoor: there is the jagged coastline, the waterfall that is higher than Niagara Falls, the bright yellow gorse bushes that are alive with linnet, the heather that changes colour, like a catwalk, with the seasons. And while the coast attracts families with small children, on the moor you merely get red-faced old couples, swathed in oilskins as if at sea.

The new boyfriend. Is there one? Is there? Or will I just give up, start wearing a scratchy tweed skirt, and allow all the veins on my face to burst? Will the fashionista finally go feral?

CHAPTER 1

* * *

(In which I realise I'm doomed!)

After a fraught four-hour drive from London, with Snoopy in his basket on the front seat glaring at me accusingly, Sweetie, Susie and Squeaks on the back seat, all in a row, heads bobbing, like the Three Degrees, I finally, after following the raging, bubbling River Exe and then the River Barle for about an hour, in a blizzard of falling red, gold and burnt umber leaves, turn into a lane, my lane. The hedgerows are full of bright green ferns, and brambles scratch at the side of my BMW convertible; I don't know whether to be cross or pleased. The middle of the lane is muddy and full of grass, which I take as a good sign. No one ever comes this way, I think. When I was deciding whether or not to buy the house, and wondering if it would be safe for my cats, the lane was, I thought, the next best thing to a moat. No one will ever find me. I can, at last, be completely and utterly on my own.

I bump across a cattle grid and am now, officially, in Exmoor National Park. I should, I suppose, shout

'Hurrah!' But instead I merely wind down my window and stick my head out into the cold, crisp air. I breathe in, slowly. I can taste a mixture of earth, moss, leaf mould and some sort of cow. It's now five in the evening and almost dark. I set off again and after a few miles I come to a fork in the road. I stick the car in neutral. I think, Jesus, it's foggy, I'm *doomed*, but then realise it's just my exhaust fumes. I am literally (well, not literally, but almost) at a crossroads in my life. I take the left fork, with its rickety sign that points to not only my new farm but to my brand-new life, and crunch slowly, tentatively, beneath a disused railway bridge and start my climb up a steep, treacherous hill, excitement mounting in my chest like a burp. I turn left again and arrive at the five-bar gate. My gate. I stop the car, get out, carefully closing my car door in case my cats, Houdini-fashion, escape from their cages and run for the hills. I open the gate. I crunch along the drive, taking in the oak trees ('My oak trees!') and sycamores ('My sycamores!') and horse chestnuts and park in an old bit of barn that's leaning ominously. ('How nice not to drive round and round for hours looking for a place to park! This is so easy!') I decide to leave the cats safely locked in the car for now, and walk up to the house. Everything is pretty gloomy. I teeter on the cobbles and see a man with a clipboard hopping by the front porch.

'Welcome!' the man shouts with what turns out to be false cheer; he looks about 12. He's the estate agent. I notice there are sheep in my fields, which are so green they are fluorescent and hurt my eyes. 'Why are there sheep in my fields?' I ask him, as he unlocks the door, which is huge, wooden and ancient. And scuffed. There are sheep skulls hung in the porch. The house, which back in the August sunshine had looked charming and olde worlde, covered in ivy, with stone mullion windows, now looks as though it's about to fall down. Why hadn't I noticed this when I looked round? I had, as usual, been living in a fantasy world rather than taking in all the details. I was already acting out a rural dream, with Cath Kidston watering cans, imagining only where I would put flowery outdoor furniture and the wooden trug I had just bought for £150 from Petersham Nurseries. I had thought that winter in the country would be romantic. I have, after all, a great deal of cashmere. I'm suddenly quite scared, and daunted. I think of my cats in the car, wrestled from their lovely warm life in London with hammocks on the beautiful cast-iron radiators, and I'm almost overcome with a weight of responsibility on my shoulders. I feel incredibly alone.

We go into the kitchen, our footsteps echoing on the filthy flagstone floors. It's freezing, and it smells – I recognise the damp aroma you get when you arrive at a villa in Tuscany, or enter an unloved church. I walk over and touch the Aga. Stone bloody freezing. I touch a radiator. As cold as a corpse. I wander into the living room and notice that the fire grate, the one I had loved and pictured myself sitting next to, has gone. The house is in darkness and no matter how many times I flick on switches – they are round and old and brown, like nipples, with twisted fabric wiring snaking down the walls – nothing happens. It turns out the previous owner has taken all the light fittings. The lovely chandelier on the stairs has been ripped in two; a bit of chain dangles sadly from the stained ceiling.

'I'm awfully sorry,' the young man says, sensing my dismay. 'They should have mentioned the Aga hasn't worked for years, and by the way they took quite a few plants from the garden, as well as the weathervane from the top of the stable block, and the stone sink you loved so much in the tack room.' I notice there is no fridge, no washing machine, no tumble dryer. All have been ripped from their moorings, leaving ghastly gashes. I go upstairs and notice the dirt, the disgusting toilets, the rusty bath, the ivy growing on the inside of the windows (who needs house plants when you have damp and mould?), and the peeling, circa 1973 Laura Ashley wallpaper (oh for the hand-printed black and white Timorous Beasties artwork I had pasted on my walls back in Gibson Square!).

'Where is my bloody furniture?' I wail, as the young man keeps striking matches. I realise I don't have any candles, or even a torch. What on earth was I thinking?

'Ah. They phoned to say they couldn't get under the disused railway bridge. Even if they had got under the bridge, they would never have got up that hill or through that mud.'

I sit down on the stairs. There's no welcoming note from the previous owner, not even a scrap of paper saying, 'Bin men Mondays'. The estate agent, despite the fact I've paid a fortune for this dump, has given me one of those awful candles with oranges stuck on the side. Oh, what I would've given for a bottle of champagne at this point.

I had left my house sparkling, with a lifetime guarantee for every appliance stashed in the American fridge, weighted down with a bottle of Mumms. I had left on the counter a laminated list of useful information, such as the name of the lady next door, the precise day and time the recycling is collected, and instructions on how to use the central heating (you can have different temperatures in every room), the wireless sound system, the Living Space Italian wardrobe that lights up so cheerfully when you open it, the elaborate outdoor lighting that also illuminates the water feature, complete with fish (I left six months' supply of fish food in one of my seamless kitchen cabinets). I left behind the Georgian fire grates, and the antique lights in the hall and stairways.

I don't know what to do. I want to travel back in time, change my mind. I had lain awake in my lovely bedroom night after night, agonising over this decision. Why hadn't I listened to my inner voice, to my instincts, to my guardian angels? Why didn't they speak up? The young man leaves – I almost hang onto his shirt tails – obviously afraid of me. He carefully places the box of matches on the step. I creep out to the car and, two by two, collect the pussy cats. I realise I don't even have an electric kettle, so I can't fill a hot-water bottle, not that I have one.

CHAPTER 2

* * *

(In which I try not to be bitter)

It had taken until the service station at Reading for the tears to stop falling messily down my face and for Snoopy to cease the mournful, open-mouthed wailing that tears at my heart, causing me to excrete the same sort of guilty, panic-stricken hormones that mothers summon up at the sound of their own crying baby. I had repeated to myself, over and over again, 'What on earth am I doing?' I was racked with doubt, and as my car ate up the miles and I found myself further and further from London, I became more and more terrified, gripping the wheel harder and harder, almost compelled to just take the next exit and turn the car around.

I had left my husband at the kerbside of Gibson Square in Islington, such a beautiful square with horse chestnut trees and blossom in spring and original black railings. I had watched his body receding in my rear-view mirror, hands shoved down hard into his pockets, forcing the elasticated waistband of his grey, elephantine sweat pants even closer to his knees, until I had seen him dip his head, turn and walk away. He hadn't even waited for my car to turn the corner and disappear from view. 'Why are you crying?' he had asked when he'd emerged from the back seat, having kissed each of the cats goodbye on their tiny heads, bumping his head in the process. 'Ow! Bugger. You don't have to leave.'

But I did have to leave. I had sold my house, my beautiful Georgian house, the perfect, pristine house I had wanted almost my whole life, with its wide, honeyed floorboards, grand fireplaces, basement kitchen with stainless-steel central island unit and underfloor heating beneath a limestone floor, Philippe Stark bathroom with its egg-shaped bath, brown marble wet room and patio garden that was so manageably small I could (and very often did) Hoover it. Why had I even put it on the market? Why had I let it slip from my grasp so easily?

Well, I did so in a fit of pique. I wanted my life to change, and change for good. I had tried living the perfect, metropolitan life. Sixty-quid organic meals for two in gastro pubs where the staff, despite the fact you have eaten there three times a week for the past decade, fail to recognise you or even acknowledge your existence; every time I sat down with my husband they would take my credit card, just in case I broke the habit of a lifetime and ran into the night before the apple crumble. There were the jaunts to Space NK on Upper Street where the over made-up young shop assistants would put by cutting-edge beauty products for me; I thought nothing of spending £47 on a candle and £700 on a 'lifting serum'; sags are worse than wrinkles, I find. I had once gone to report on the Oscars, and been invited to choose something from the Versace store on Rodeo Drive. The dwarf-like male shop assistant had made me laugh by saying, 'Have you ever said hello to a heel? Ah,' he exclaimed as he saw my face brighten, 'a smile is nature's face lift!'

I hadn't had much to smile about recently. Oh, I loved wandering home with armfuls of white flowers from the stall next to St Peter's Church that I would then place carefully on the floor by the fireplace next to the French windows. I loved jumping into a cab on Old Bond Street knowing I'd be home in a jiffy. I loved the fact that, every Friday morning, the Indian man from the dry cleaner round the corner would turn up on my doorstep to take away my bed linen, and return it later all pressed and lovely and wrapped in crisp white paper. The dry-cleaning man once referred to my husband as 'your son' and very nearly lost my business; only the prospect of ironing the sheets made me hold my tongue. I loved walking round the corner to the Screen on the Green, watching a film, then wandering back to my house, seeing its first floor lights twinkling, showing the dusky pink walls and amazing central light (an upside-down firework of bulbs), and being proud that this was my home. That I did it. Yay! That all the hard work, the long hours toiling away at the shallow (i.e. life and style) end of a Sunday newspaper (I started out as a sub-editor on the TV pages; my three-line summaries of the fare on offer on Sky were perfect haikus) were worth it. I'd made it. I should've been happy, but I would often wish that I was a Buddhist, so my happiness came from within, unaffected by outside forces.

I had everything I needed to make me content: success, friends, a certain sort of fame in some circles. Everything, in fact, except a husband who loved me.

I'm trying, very, very hard, to put what he did behind me, hence, of course, the 200-mile relocation to the other side of the country. And so I will attempt to be brief, not to inject too much bile (fat bastard!) into my sentences, as I tell you what happened. I will try not to put, in brackets, the words (poor me!) at too frequent intervals. I will try to be fair. Above all, I will try not to be bitter (fat bloody bastard!).

I don't think it would be fair to say we were ever happy, but we rubbed along, me frantically smoothing his path like a matronly woman in a white coat at a particularly heated game of curling. I worked, first on the Sunday newspaper, later as the editor of a women's magazine, while he lazed around at home in sportswear ostensibly writing his first 'novel' (a thinly disguised autobiography, embellished with frequent sexual conquests), but in fact wreaking revenge on me for earning more than he did, and for loving him, even though he didn't even like himself that much. I had often thought he was a casebook socio-path, unable to empathise when I would crawl through the front door, exhausted from yet another day spent down a mine, or at least in a newspaper office. On reflection, I realise he was just suffering from chronically low self-esteem.

I would involve him in my world as much as I could. Quite early on in our relationship I took him with me to New York. We stayed at the SoHo Grand, and I told him he was free to kick his heels and explore while I attended the ready-to-wear shows; he'd never been to New York before. I think I even gave him spending money as he had only come with £20 in his pocket. I thought it odd that, when I would whizz back to the room to change (I had pulled numerous strings to get a suite with a view of the Empire State Building), he would always be tucked up in bed, just in his pants, watching porn. I took him to meet my glamorous friend Emma for dinner, and on the last night I took him to the Calvin Klein fashion show in a huge warehouse, where he got to sit in the front row. Only years later did he tell me he had 'felt like a trophy, a bit of Indian fluff to have on your arm'. Which wasn't how I had meant it at all: I thought he'd like gazing at perfect, youthful, hairless buttocks just inches from his nose. It seemed we would misfire, miscommunicate, throughout our marriage, him taking anything nice done by me as some sort of attack. Ah well.

I later found out that the marriage was littered with his nasty little excursions, right from the word go. There were women he met at parties – I know about one little cow called Jess, but I'm sure there were others – while leaving me at home, or abroad working, or sat late at night at my desk. I didn't even have a clue about the yoga teachers he had pursued, like a lovesick puppy, while I had thought he was merely trying to get back in shape (fat bastard!) and become more flexible. Looking back, I think how stupid I was to send him to Ibiza for a week's yoga retreat – I even drove him to Stansted Airport! I should have behaved like other women do with their husbands: bossed him relentlessly, made him pay for things, value me more. It was a recipe for disaster, leaving him at home to write his book.

It all came out, of course it did, like an abscess after a soak in Epsom salts. I received an email after we broke up from a female former friend of his, and in it she wrote, 'N was always "in love" with someone. Once, when you came home from work and he was on the phone to me and he took the phone upstairs, he was gushingly telling me he was in love with his yoga instructor who, sensible girl, had told him more than once she wasn't interested, but he didn't believe her and was practically stalking her!' I got to the point where I couldn't take any more of these emails. Take this one: 'I have always thought you were rather cool, despite what your husband used to say about you.' What? What did he say? Apparently, he had long planned to call his second 'novel' *White Bitch*. How nice. Ye godfathers. Why didn't these people tell me at the time? Why now, when it's too late?

When I found out that he was being unfaithful, having affairs with six different women on a three-month trip to his homeland, India, while awaiting publication of his 'novel', in a way it was a relief. There was a reason for his distance, his moods, our lack of sex; rather than just being odd, or gay (the thought had crossed my mind); at least he was behaving in a textbook case of philandering. I found out about 'Daphne' (her real name) by reading his text messages one Christmas Eve while he was in the shower, only a month after he had got back from India. 'It was great to see you yesterday. I'll get to New York as soon as I can,' he had written. 'Your toes are as cute as the rest of you. N x.'

Had I known, somewhere deep inside of me, that he was being unfaithful? While he was away, I knew something wasn't right by the tone of his voice, the brevity of his emails. He seemed sad, completely disinterested in what I might be doing. I understand now that, when he sounded sad, he was just covering up for euphoria. I phoned him once to tell him I was in the middle of an earthquake in Pakistan, and I could just tell he was with someone. 'I've got a minute,' was all he would say, as if I had been describing how I'd just popped out to buy some Fairy Liquid. Isn't the point of being married having someone who cares about what you are doing, that your bed might be see-sawing across a hotel room? He ended our one-sided conversation with the damning, 'You take care.'

When he finally came out of the shower, I was standing there, holding his phone. He looked at my hand, then carried on drying his iron filings hair with my nice towel.

'Have you met someone?'

'No.'

'Who's Daphne?'

He actually smiled to himself, as if he were hugging a treasured memory and didn't want to lose sight of it. I wanted to stab him.

I chucked him out, literally. He might have been fat but I can really shove when I want to. I was shouting at him so loudly I frightened Susie, who broke the cat flap in her haste to escape. I threw all his supermarket own-brand possessions into the street after him. I heard him calling his friend Pattie, asking her to pick him up. He's the sort of man who always needs help, to involve other people in his mess. When she arrived, I opened the door and almost spat at her. 'Thanks for telling me he was fucking someone else. Fucking feminist you are.' She didn't answer. I'd never liked her. She's the sort of woman who thinks being a mother deserves some sort of medal, and reverence, and expensive gifts. Honestly, who gives a birthday party for a one-year-old and invites all her adult friends? Why did she never dress her child in any of the clothes I bought it? Why? Why?

I took him back within three days. 'Oh Baby, I love you so much!' he had sobbed down the phone and I had weakened. I actually drove to Pattie's house to load back into my car all the things I had tossed out onto the pavement. When we got home, he just left everything in the hallway for months. His bike stayed on the roof of my car for two weeks. Isn't it interesting, though, what a little motivation can do for even the most languorous, disorganised of men? I now know that the day before Christmas Eve, when he had got up at 6 am, put on the charcoal Helmut Lang sweater I had bought him in Paris and hurried out the door, ostensibly off to a 'meeting' (what 'novelist' does meetings?), he was in fact on his way to see Daphne. How ironic that I had, drowsily, offered to drive him to the Tube station. It's to his (slight) credit that he had turned me down. I remember when he got home that night he had tried to make love to me, but he had such a weird look in his eye – was it pity, nostalgia? – I had pushed him away.

After he moved back in, he whisked me away to New York for a weekend. Well, not whisk, exactly. He had to borrow my credit card to book the room at the Hudson – horrid, trendy, noisy place at the wrong end of town – and the plane tickets. Plus, I was suspicious he was simply not allowing his own plane ticket go to waste (he had told Daphne he would be there as soon as he could, so had bought a ticket already), and besides, I travel there so often for work, it wasn't really the treat he thought it was. You see how I was difficult, too?

I know now, of course, that part of the reason I took him back was that I wanted more details. I wanted to find out what she had that I didn't, aside from being born 10 years later. One night, while he was asleep, the duvet stuffed between his thighs, one pillow folded in half and punched, the other tossed on the floor (*oh my god*, he was so *annoying*), I took his camera into the spare room and scrolled through the pictures he had taken in India. At first there were all the usual touristy snaps – the Golden Temple, the lakes at Udaipur. And then, there she was. Daphne. Walking in front of him, barefoot and almost beautiful, turning to smile over her shoulder. Sat in a bikini on a balcony overlooking water. The picture that hurt the most and that I stared at the longest was the close-up of her in bed, asleep, a collection of colourful strings around her narrow, tanned wrist. I deleted them all, one by one. He never commented on my Stalinist actions; he had been too lazy to delete the photos,

I imagine he was too lazy to ever look at them. Months later, I would wish I had kept them, so that I could study her face for flaws, remind myself of his betrayal, torture myself and him just a little bit more thoroughly.

We ticked along, with just one blip. I had been manically monitoring him, checking his texts several times a day (he would actually hand over his phone without a murmur), but then one day, going through his wallet, I found her passport picture. I sat it on the kitchen table, next to his wallet, and when he saw it he didn't say a word: he just picked it up and popped it back in next to his Tube pass and driving licence. The following September – on my *birthday*, would you believe – he had taken me out for dinner at what turned out to be a sandwich bar. When we got home, I sat down at my computer (he had, as usual, turned on the telly the moment we got in) and realised he was still logged onto his email. It was a hotmail account, not his usual BT one, and I noticed his username was 'Puppy', the name of the hero and alter ego in his 'novel'. I didn't say anything, trying to remain calm, and clicked on the unopened envelope at the top of the queue. I heard the sea in my ears. It was from the dreaded Daphne, asking friskily, 'N, are we still meeting in New York next week?'

'Why is Daphne writing to you?'

I'll never forget the look on his face. It was like Snoopy's when he realises he's off-target with the litter tray. He rushed over to where I was sat and tried to lean over me to get to the keyboard. I shoved him, hard, jabbing him with my elbows; he had always said that sleeping with me was like being in bed with a broken umbrella, or a deckchair: all hard angles. As he stood there, hovering nervously, almost hopping on the spot in his holey, worn Adidas socks (you never dress up for me, even on my birthday, I had thought at that moment), I clicked on each email in turn. He had sent the first back in July, telling her he thought about her 'every single day'. I remembered that day. I had been at Ladies' Day at Ascot, reporting on the hats, and he hadn't called me once, even though I had left at dawn and was gone for what seemed like light years. When I'd got home, exhausted, hungry, he was sat at his desk in his 'office', and could barely lift his eyelids to look at me. Now I know why. Now I know why.

In one email, he wrote to tell her he was watching the World Cup and was supporting Germany. 'What, you're fucking a German?' I shouted, Basil Fawlty popping into my consciousness. They had arranged to meet in London – 'Ah, so that's why you wouldn't come to Sussex with me that week' – but she had cancelled at the last minute, afraid she would upset her photographer boyfriend. 'My God,' I said finally, 'she's a whore. Why did you contact her again when you swore to me you wouldn't?'

'I felt bad that I had ended it the way I did. I wanted to see how she was doing. I wanted to feel good about myself.'

'Doesn't being with me make you feel that?'

He looked down at his giant feet and didn't answer. He once said I never paid him a compliment. 'Yes I did,' I replied. 'I once remarked that your feet are like paddles, so you must be able to swim well.' Maybe I was more cruel than I would like to believe I was.

I hated that he had done this to me, that he'd lied, that he had thought so little of me, the person who was supposed to be the most important in his life, and I hated that he had tipped me into a cliché. I blamed myself as well, for not really loving him as much as I could have done, not fancying him as much as I had my previous boyfriend, Kevin the Osama Bin Laden lookalike, a musician who looms large in my memory but who, in reality, I only went out with about three times. I played the wounded wife, and after we had argued until three in the morning, him sobbing and sobbing, me saying I had to go to bed to get up for work – 'I don't have time for this!' – I let him stay. But that night in September when he cried and I thumped him with his trainers, I fell out of love with him. 'Why?' I had asked him that night, 'if you didn't want me, couldn't you have just said so? Why make my life worthless, a lie?' I thought of all his friends – Pattie, the friends he met while travelling – who knew about Daphne, who had sat in my house, on my nice sofas, and all the time they were laughing at me. How dare he mire me in his sordid, deceitful, self-obsessed life?

CHAPTER 3

* * *

(In which I think, my God, he's not even that attractive. How do these people do it?)

In a way, from that point our marriage became a sort of sport. I wanted to see if I could make him love me more than any other woman, if I could win him back, if I could keep him away from the dreaded Daphne. I gave him blow jobs on demand and didn't even stop when one of my sharp back teeth caused an ulcer. 'Do you,' I said to him once, looking up into his fat face as he sat at the kitchen table watching interracial porn on my laptop, 'even know that I'm here?'

In a way it was gratifying, that he didn't end up with Daphne, a stupid Manhattanite ('Hi, how are yeeeeeww?' is all they know how to say; in my many years spent working on magazines setting up shoots with Hollywood stars, I have yet to come across an American female who even knows how to dial an outside line) who is probably now, as I type, waggling her white broderie anglaise maxi skirt-clad bottom at somebody else's husband. Her emails made me cringe. I knew my husband would have hated her terrible grammar and lack of self-awareness. She would write about the fact she was 'working out every day' and wittered on about how she 'wants to give something back to India' and 'work for a not-for-profit organisation'. This from a woman who was working for a conglomerate that had set up a casino in the heat of apartheid. From that moment forward I referred to her as 'the travel agent'.

The final nail in the coffin of our so-called marriage (you see? He made me act out a bloody cliché) was when we were on holiday on a small island called Vamizi off the coast of Mozambique and I realised, as I watched him being ferried in a small boat in turquoise, 30-degree water to go scuba diving for the day, how miserable we were. I'd stayed on dry land having gagged at the thought of having a big, tubular object in my mouth; isn't it weird how your body, despite years of conditioning that 'I must have a boyfriend', will ultimately rebel; I'm so, so glad I don't have to perform fellatio any more. I took his picture on the Canon camera I had bought him to go travelling with. He had sent me an email from Mumbai complaining that it was so big and heavy it made him 'hot'. I peered at his image in the tiny screen, at his body encased in black rubber, and realised the expression on his face resembled that of a child on its way to a concentration camp.

Two weeks before our African holiday, he had returned from promoting his 'novel' in India in a foul mood, opening the fridge door repeatedly, only to stare inside furiously and not take anything out. Later that day I checked his phone, and saw a text he had sent to his friend Ashley, saying: 'I'm moving out. Fancy renting a flat with me?' I threatened him a few days before departure, actually grabbing a handful of his T-shirt and saying, through gritted, recently re-veneered teeth, that he 'had better not bloody well ruin it or I will demand you pay me back for your half'. You see? Never look after men or pay for things because they will only grow to hate you. My fantasy during our marriage was that I would die in a car crash and he would inherit my life insurance, and would at last be all grateful and filled with remorse at my funeral. Having taken the picture of him sat slumped in the boat and seen the misery etched on his face, that night in the huge four-poster bed I had to know what was going on.

'What the bloody hell is wrong with you?' I shouted, confronted, yet again, by his wide brown back. I tried to flounce away from him and got caught up in the mosquito net, only making myself madder. 'Did you sleep with someone at the Mumbai literary festival?'

'No, I didn't sleep with anyone.'

'Did you think about sleeping with someone? I know something happened. One minute you were fine on the phone, chatty, normal, the next you kept giving me those ominous, pregnant pauses you're so fond of.'

'No, I didn't think about sleeping with someone else, but I thought about you, a lot. I thought about how you were always complaining, telling me about the Oscars when I was surrounded by starving children. Listening to you banging on was boring.'

'Oh,' I didn't say, but the thought raced through my head like Carl Lewis, 'play the bloody working-class race card, why don't you? This is all fine and dandy from a man who on our walking holiday in the poorest state in India only got £10 out of the machine at Heathrow Airport, and returned two weeks later with £5 and some £2 coins in his bastard pocket.'

'Oh, give me a break,' I said out loud. 'You're the boring one, you self-obsessed fat bastard.'

'Her name was mumble mumble.'

'Pardon?' I forgot to mention that I'm quite deaf, and usually get by with lip reading and guesswork. As my husband had turned his big fat head away from me at this point, his words were muffled by the squashy pillow.

'K*****!' He spat out her name.

'Don't shout at me!' I said, my lower lip quivering. 'Spell it.'

He spelt it. How stupid, I thought, are you to spell her name – I can Google her and get her email address. I was already looking forward to what I was going to say to her. (I've just looked at her picture on Facebook and laughed at her big fat arse and stupid face and enormous nose and worryingly low hairline.)

He told me she had been one of the authors at the festival (from that moment on, I only ever referred to her as 'the work experience girl') and had turned up at his hotel to lend him some books, only to 'come on to me'. He had the cheek to smirk at this point. 'Oh my God, she was so dirty,' he said, smiling at the memory. 'These Indian girls, they look so pure and innocent, they are so sweet and shiny-haired and good to their mums, but my God, the things she wanted me to do to her.'

Part of me wanted to scream at him and hit him, while another part was thinking, 'My God, how do these men do it? He's not even that attractive. I spent my entire twenties and thirties without so much as a snog, and I was reasonably good-looking, well dressed, thin, *available.*'

I couldn't, then or now, quite work out why he was telling me this, only three days into our holiday, so far away from home that we had had to get there on three planes of diminishing size, and then a sail boat. I wondered if it might be that he was feeling trapped, given we were on an island. Then I figured out that he was actually pleased with himself: it was exactly like Sweetie bringing in a shrew and placing it on my pillow with a look that says, 'Aren't I clever, Mummy?'

'Did you use a condom?'

'No.'

'She might be pregnant.' I didn't know, as I said this, whether I meant her being pregnant was a stunning achievement that he would welcome and I'd be jealous of, given the antiquity of my own ovaries, which had for some time been sitting in deckchairs in Eastbourne and wondering whether to have some Battenberg cake or make do with a custard cream, or as a threat, knowing how he hates to be tied down. Even in our first year of marriage he would hate it if I seemed too keen and demanding, asking what he might be doing on a Saturday afternoon. 'Why?' he would say cagily, suspiciously.

'I didn't come inside her.'

For several hours, I told him how disgusted he made me feel. He smoked endless cigarettes that he had blagged off the waiters, stubbing them out in a pile in the perfect, pristine sand. He begged me to let him stay so that we could carry on talking. 'We could sit by the ocean and get to know each other again,' he said. 'That's how we fell in love, in Jamaica, during Euro 2000. We could fall in love again.'

I stood up. I was glad it was dark because I hate having an argument when I'm not wearing make-up. 'Pack your rucksack, get out of my villa and leave,' I said. He looked surprised. I marched off to the bar, its twinkly lights and squashy white cushions mocking me. Later, the manager of the resort, speaking softly and empathetically, told me she had put my husband in another villa and that he would be leaving the next morning. I remember thinking, How will he pay the fare or have the dollars ready for his exit visa? I realised I had, in fact, turned into his mother, or at least his holiday rep. I later got a message saying he had taken my passport by mistake and could he do a swap in the morning at breakfast? I thought this was an elaborate ruse to see me again, to fall at my feet and clutch my ankles but, then again, he had probably just been careless. Only he could take a passport from a safe and be happy with only a 50/50 chance of it being the right one. I left his behind the bar.

As soon as I saw his small plane lift into the pale sky the next morning I emailed my solicitor (I had obtained the number of a divorce firm during the looking-in-the-fridge episodes) while I remained on the island, alone, pitied at meal times by all the honeymooning couples, and told her to file for divorce, citing K*****, and to instruct my husband to be out of my house by the time I returned. I was relieved that he was going back and would be able to take over cat-sitting duties from H, my cleaner. I emailed K***** as well, telling her I knew she had had unprotected sex with my husband, and perhaps she would like to make her Muslim boyfriend aware of that fact before he read about it in my column in a Sunday news-paper. She emailed back to say she had reported me to the Press Complaints Commission. All I had wanted was a simple 'I'm sorry'. God, even the dreaded Daphne, when I had emailed her, asking whether she was aware she was 'number five out of the six women he had sex with in India', had had the good grace to apologise and tell my husband not to contact her again. I hacked into my husband's email (I knew he would be too lazy to change his password), and saw that he had already forewarned K*****, apologising (!) profusely, saying he had no idea why 'Liz has blown this all out of proportion'. Why is he on her side, I wailed to no one in particular. Why was he never on mine?

Ten days later, I stepped out of my black cab from the airport, all brown and flip-flopped, and as I put the key in the door I almost hoped he was still there, smiling and apologetic. Because I'd never had a proper boyfriend, let alone someone who had said, at first, that he loved me, I suppose there was a small part of me that thought a man in my life, even a bastard one, was better than nothing at all. But he wasn't there. The hallway was bereft of his bicycle, which had annoyed me by dripping oil on the floorboards and snagging my cardis, but which I now missed. I walked through each room, the subtle voids not immediately evident until I got to the top floor and his lovely office, with its steel 1920s desk and Eames swivel chair and Nicole Farhi squashy club chair for when he wanted to 'just read' (nap), and I saw that the book shelves were full of yawning gaps, like a tramp's mouth. His meditation stool was gone. I'm afraid at that moment I buckled.

I placed a block on his emails after he sent me this: 'You freely married an unemployed man 16 [!] years your junior. No one forced or lied you into it. You pissed on your last chance at happiness. I will have others. So the final laugh is mine.' Who had said I was laughing? Bored one night, though, I decided to Google him, and came across a radio interview he gave in which the (extremely flirtatious, blonde) female presenter challenged him, pointing out that his laziness and infidelity and pre-dilection for calling me 'Chubby' must have caused me a lot of mental anguish. And he had replied, 'She had plenty of problems before I came along, trust me.'

But isn't the point of being married that you help each other with your problems and your hang-ups, not exacerbate them, rub at them and make them sore, like a particularly bad case of athlete's foot? And anyway, was I really, really that bad? It was slightly gratifying that, when we did finally start talking again after he moved out, he told me that, having dated a few crackpots since splitting up with me, he had realised I am, in fact, commendably normal. His first girlfriend on getting back to London from Africa was a struggling writer who sent him topless pictures of herself; ye gods, I was too shy to even phone him to let him know I was on my way home from work, and he was my husband! 'Perhaps things would have been different if you hadn't been the first woman I fell in love with,' he said at one point, 'and instead were the last, after I'd got all the crap ones out the way.'

Oh, he tried to win me back, of course he did. He left me a voice message that, sadly, I listened to over and over again. I wish I'd kept it so I could listen to it now. 'We can take it slowly. I had dinner with David S the other night at the organic pub and I told him that you are, with all certainty, the love of my life. I can give you space. I could use my flat [hovel] in Camden as an office. I'd forgotten how sexy you look in that black suit. Don't leave me dangling, Fatty.'

Why wouldn't he want me back? I was nice. I was well groomed and wore expensive clothes. I had a BMW convertible that he used to take out on jaunts even though he hadn't bothered to find out how to switch the head-lights on ('How d'you do it, Lizzie?' he had shouted down his mobile late one night; I found out later he'd had a woman with him at the time. Who did she think I was, I wonder, his maiden aunt, his mechanic, Jeremy Clarkson?). I had taken him on exotic holidays – in chronological order: Jamaica (Ian Fleming's house, to be precise), Thailand (we stayed in Leonardo DiCaprio's suite; he had, unfortunately, vacated it), the Cotswolds,

Puglia, Marrakech (where I had a migraine and threw up, plus I didn't like the way they kept the horses up late at night and let off guns next to them), New York (on our second visit we stayed in the Mandarin Oriental Hotel with its view of Central Park and rooftop pool; 'I've forgotten my goggles,' he'd whined like a baby in a wet nappy), Paris (the Costes, which is so dark I wandered around groping the walls like Roy Orbison), Udaipur, Mauritius, Uttaranchal and Florence, where he'd splashed me in the infinity pool. 'My eyes! My eyes!' I'd wailed ... Looking back, my stab at happiness had been an expensive joke, hadn't it?

I know now the whole marriage was, as far as he was concerned, a sick exercise in opportunism; that he just used me from the word go. I waited all my life for him, and I find out now that I was never really loved, not properly, not like my dad loved my mum. He might have said I was the love of his life, but what are words worth, really? I told him I didn't care how he felt, I cared how he made *me* feel. I asked my friend Emine what she thought and she said she believed he was with me for the nice lifestyle. Nobody could be that cruel or mercenary, could they? I can hardly believe I had someone like that in my life, and that he was telling so many people he was 'in love' with someone else. Why didn't one of them bother to tell me? I have nothing to look back on and cherish, I don't have the consolation of knowing that I was, even once, fleetingly adored. Even on our wedding night I couldn't find him and went to bed in our great big hotel suite alone, worrying. Who does that, honestly? The next morning, to pile insult upon injury, when I woke he was already up, dressed and gone, not having even left a note. I found him having a full English breakfast with one of his lesbian friends, this despite the fact that a) it was our wedding boxing day; and b) he had told me he was a vegetarian.

I suppose the question I keep asking over and over again in my head is, why did I put up with him for so long? Why did I allow myself to be treated in this way? Why, when he behaved badly, did I try harder to improve myself, to make myself so impossible to resist and generous and nice that he would 'come round', as it were. I've always had shockingly low self-esteem − remember I mentioned those mid-Seventies discos? I was always ignored by boys and didn't get my first boyfriend until I was 30. Shameful, isn't it? I suppose I felt I didn't deserve someone who didn't require an enormous amount of payment/patience/presents from me to keep him interested. I have to admit, as well, that I didn't want to break up with him until I was the best that I could be, so that he would remember me in a really good light.

I knew I had to get rid of him, that he would cheat on me again, despite his tearful protestations to the contrary when I found out about Daphne, but I waited until I had bought the new house, had the wallpapering and decorating done, until I had had more work done on my teeth to make them perfect (I'm not being untruthful here when I say my teeth could be in the movies), got nice and brown on holiday in Africa, and then I thought, okay, it doesn't get any better than this, why don't you leave now before I start wearing bifocals and crocheting doilies to place on the backs of three-piece suites?

After the island confession we had not spoken or communicated except via my solicitor – he was too lazy to hire one of his own and so he sort of shared mine – but then he called me, ostensibly to enquire after the cats. He kept asking if he could visit Snoopy. I tried to persuade him to come round while H was there so that I could avoid him, but this was just a half-hearted attempt to show I wasn't interested. And so, late one night, he turned up at my door. We were careful with each other. We padded down to the kitchen. He stood around, looking as he always did – an uncomfortable guest in his own home – and then he hugged me. We ended up having sex on the brown leather sofa from SCP on Curtain Road. I had spotted him moments before lowering the blinds (you thought I was going to say 'lowering his trousers', didn't you? That would have been far too obvious) onto the street, and so I guessed what was on his mind. 'I knew we would end up having sex the moment I heard your voice,' he said. 'And then the way you just lit up, like a bulb, when you saw me.' Later, we sat in the living room and he looked around as though seeing the room for the first time and said, 'It's so beautiful here. I never really saw it before [you see? I can read him like a book], or appreciated it. Or you. I was blind, I suppose. I was full of rage and resentment. Don't sell this house. I don't think we should get divorced.'

For his 33rd birthday, I treated him to dinner at the

Cinnamon Club in Victoria and he actually, I kid ye not, went to sit at another table to read his book. I realised he could only bear to be in my company for as long as it took to eat a vegetable samosa.

CHAPTER 4

* * *

(In which I know I would have weakened. His Woolworths duvet didn't even have a cover!)

The truth is, I would have taken him back, but I didn't want to still be with him when I turned 50, less than two years away. I dreaded to think, couldn't face, how he would treat me then. The jokes about me breaking my hip, the cries of 'Come on, old lady!' would doubtless have increased in frequency. One of our ill-fated 'dates' during this limbo period ended with us sat in my car outside the house, him yelling in my ear, 'You fucking hag! You fucking old hag!'

He sent me an email the next day to apologise. 'You were a brilliant wife in so many ways,' he said. 'No one will love me as much as you have, and nor will I ever love anyone as much as I love you . . . it is proof of what a mess I am that I behaved the way I did to the person who has meant more to me than anyone. I have no idea what makes me the way I am. I do wish you well. And thank you for letting me see the cats. They were beautiful – as ever. I will miss you all dreadfully.'

Why didn't he write that *I* was beautiful? Why? Why?

One day, about three months after he'd moved out, sitting in that huge, overstuffed Nicole Farhi chair, I realised that this, all of this, was not enough. There was only so much fiddling with the precise location of my numerous Rastafarian floor cushions I could do. Now that I had my life back, and was able to liberate my clothes and use both sides of my lovely Italian wardrobe that lights up when you slide open a door, I had started to think, what next? Do I just sit here in my lovely house? And do what, exactly? I knew, too, that I was weakening, feeling sorry for him living in his basement flat (hovel) in Camden, with his thin Woolworths duvet that didn't even have a cover, and his single, solitary pillow, as flat as a pancake.

And so I persuaded myself that I wanted to start again, to throw all this away and prove – to him? To myself? – a point: namely, that I'm not shallow or materialistic; that I don't need all the glamour of London and the masseuse who will come with her table on a Friday evening just because I'm feeling tired and stressed. I don't need the exquisite hand-blown things from Atelier Abigail Aherne (well, I do sort of still need them; I took them with me anyway) because none of them made me feel at peace. And, to be honest, London had started to get on my nerves. Not just the expense, or the fact I was always getting parking tickets or having the wheels on my BMW stolen, or not being able to get an appointment for a Hollywood wax at the Aveda spa (I've been known to shout down the phone: 'You're supposed to be a bloody spa, not an NHS hospital.' Honestly, I had started to hate myself). Not just the drunken, giant teenagers wobbling on children's bicycles, yelling at each other late at night outside my house (why do they have to shout 'Oy!' across the square? They have mobile phones, for chrissakes. I thought this square was supposed to be an exclusion zone!), or the fact people might be able to afford to live in a garden square but apparently not have the where-withal to clean their front steps or replace the grey, wizened specimens dying in window boxes or use proper bin bags instead of knotted Sainsbury's carrier bags.

Most of all I hated that my cats had to go out and about in a dangerous city, where who knows what might happen to them. Two weeks before I moved, just after I got back from the fashion shows in Paris, Susie went missing. I had to exchange contracts, knowing she was missing and that I couldn't possibly move without her. I printed leaflets and stuck them on every lamppost in Islington. I took out an advert on the front page of the local newspaper, a piece of folly as it meant every crank in London called my mobile at all hours of the night ('I have your cat. If you don't meet me outside Borders in half an hour I will cut off her paw.' 'Really, you're holding her, are you?' 'Yeah.' 'In your arms?' 'Yeah, I'm strokin' her right now.' 'Well, you're a liar,' I said, knowing full well no one can hold Susie in their arms for long, least of all a stranger, and I hung up). When I eventually heard her high little mew coming, at 3 am, from inside the garage of the house on the opposite corner of the square, I knocked on the door of the male couple who lived there. They refused to let me search the garage. I returned the next night at 11 pm, brandishing a bottle of vintage champagne, although I'm sure a bottle of Cava would have done; this is me, you see, all over. They reluctantly opened the garage, which was packed with rubbish. I could smell cat pee, and I knew Susie was still in there. Eventually I found her, tucked in a corner, eyes big and scared. I managed to stuff her in her basket and as I walked back to my house I made a promise to her that I would keep her safe. That I would be taking her somewhere she wouldn't be caught by feral boys, or have to listen to fireworks, or be trapped in some arsehole's untidy garage ('It's a death trap, an accident waiting to happen,' I'd said over my shoulder as I flounced off with my cat). Was falling out of love with London as well as my husband a sign of defeat? That I had decided to retire from the ring? I don't know. Maybe.

H, who always left my house ashen-faced after she had damp-dusted skirting boards and, despite great personal danger, light bulbs, had come along on my last morning to say goodbye and to help me get the last of my things in the car. My ex-husband had cycled from his basement flat (hovel) in Camden – he was, as he always is, late – ostensibly to help, but instead he just stood around, doing his uncomfortable guest impression, as if he could hardly wait to make his excuses. He had the cheek to stand there, only half listening to me, surreptitiously texting on his mobile phone. 'Hmm?' he would say, lifting, with great effort, his great big eyes from whatever was in his palm. Actually, we were still married at this point; it would be another four weeks before I received my decree nisi in the post; I filed it in the brown folder entitled 'Marriage' in my left-hand drawer, along with the sample wedding breakfast menus from Babington House (I was so anxious at my wedding I forgot to eat a piece of the organic chocolate and raspberry wedding cake), and one lone pressed cream rose, the only survivor of my posy. I had tossed it in a corner of the terrace during the champagne reception; the hotel had posted it on to me later. I think, with hindsight, this was an omen.

To get him to do something useful, H sent him out for lattes, and he was gone for about an hour, which again was something he always did: take hours and hours and hours to complete the simplest task. But this morning, I hadn't really minded. I was already feeling nostalgic for my old life, even before it had quite come to an end. I found out later that, on the day I moved out of London, he had sent an email to his new girlfriend, the exhibitionist one, telling her he was going 'to help Liz move'. Hmm, yeah, right. He was a great help. Isn't it odd, too, how people like to portray themselves to others? Maybe they believe that is who they really are, what they are really like.

The removal men, who reminded me of Abbott and Costello and whom I had seen exchanging elaborate eye rolls in the face of my hysterical demands (*'Vogues* September 1975 to October 2007 have to be kept in *strict chronological order!*), had stacked my Vi-Spring mattress ('Folded?! You don't fold a Vi-Spring!') in the back of the huge van, and already set off, beads of sweat on their foreheads. Having locked the black front door that had so recently been painted, and having enjoyed a last glimpse of my black and white Timorous Beasties wallpaper that had barely had time to dry, it was just me, my cats, H, my soon-to-be-ex-husband, my beauty products and a supply of cat food in case the removal van got lost in a mismatched huddle at the bottom of the steps. I realised this was the sum total of nearly 28 years of living, working and dreaming in London.

'It's such a beautiful house,' my ex-husband said after I'd locked the door and H had disappeared, narrow shoulders shuddering, to deliver the keys to the estate agent. I'd sold the house to an unmarried chef, baulking at the prospect of anyone with children ruining the pristine beeswaxiness of my floors.

'Why did you never appreciate it?' I asked him. 'Why didn't you ever appreciate me?'

'I don't know,' he said, shaking his head, his iron filings hair glinting in the sun. He twined his chubby fingers in mine. 'I'll miss you,' he said. 'London will miss you, too.'

It's now 10 pm, and I've installed myself in what seems, marginally, to be the warmest of the upstairs rooms. It smells like the inside of a guinea pig hutch. I've put the cats, along with their food, water and special pillows, in the big cages I brought with me as a sort of halfway house between basket and bedroom. I'm on the floor, fully clothed, with Squeaky on top of me (she is such a person I can trust her not to be in a cage with the others; she is also far too big to disappear up the chimney). All of this activity I've had to illuminate using my mobile phone which, needless to say, can't get a bloody signal. I think, with shame, that if I'd been able to get a signal I would've phoned my husband, and wailed down the phone for help and forgiveness. I don't think I've been this cold since I went skiing in Montgenèvre aged 18 and lost my gloves. Through the window I can see the moon and the stars, so many stars it's almost like being back on Vamizi. I cannot see a single light from another house. I feel tearful, alone and scared. An owl hoots outside.

And then I think to myself: I can either look at this as a disaster, and moan and whine and cry and be defeatist (the 'Poor me!' option). Or I can look at it as an adventure, a beginning, the start of something brand new and exciting, only with Glastonbury-style dirty camping thrown in at the beginning. Luckily, after a bit of thought and a great deal of umming and aaahhing and crying and asking Squeaky what she thinks, I decide to do the latter.

CHAPTER 5

* * *

(In which I blame the Pullein-Thompson sisters for how my life is turning out)

I fall in love with horses the way most women fall in love with men. I was about five when my dad drove me one Saturday morning to my first riding lesson, during which I developed my inaugural crush: a pony called Chocolate, who was small, brown (hence the name) and wilful. After a few years I then graduated to a bigger riding school in a village called Stock in Essex. My favourite pony was called Flicka: he was beautiful, with a thick black mane. His only problem was that if you touched his withers he would go bananas. As I got taller I graduated to a big, excitable bay called Cavalier who would rush his fences, ducking out at the last moment only to circle the field, flat out, like a demented greyhound. I filled the time between riding lessons by reading pony books: *Jill Has Two Ponies*, *A Stable for Jill*, *Jill's Pony Trek*, *We Hunted Hounds*, *Farewell to Hounds*, *I Wanted a Pony*, *I Had Three Ponies* and *Riders from Afar*. I loved this last book: it was about an uptight equestrian family in 1950s England who are descended upon by loud, outsize American teenagers whose parents drive a gas-guzzling Buick; I've just dug it out, and see I bastardised the title in Biro so that it reads 'Riders from Affair'; my dormant sexuality was, I suppose, lurking not too far beneath the curry comb-wielding surface. I loved the reassuring Englishness of these books, set in a world where nothing could go far wrong, not while there were words like 'smashing' and 'golly'. As a child faced with boys and homework and going out into the big bad world it was nice to remain in a cocoon of fawn ties and girls called Babs and April Cholly-Sawcutt, where ponies were sometimes 'slugs', and tea was always 'supersonic'. I suppose, as well as my ex-husband, I blame the Pullein-Thompson sisters and Ruby Ferguson, who conjured up these small, class-conscious, rural, deeply moral and sporting, spiffing worlds with kind mummies in aprons and helpful neighbouring colonels, for how my life is turning out.

As a teenager, my love of horses showed no sign of abating. Not confident enough to put on make-up and go to parties and meet boys, I preferred to spend my formative years in jodhpurs, with straw in my hair and manure under my fingernails. When I was doing my A levels I used to muck out at my local stables in exchange for rides on a chestnut called Storm. I would spend every Saturday and Sunday there, occasionally huddled in a caravan eating peanut butter sandwiches. I was never paid for all this hard work; I did it all out of love. I would make copious notes every time I rode. I still have the pile of notebooks I kept during all those years of weekly riding lessons in return for mucking out stables. They are filled with mild triumphs and wild defeats. I would carefully jot down the name of the pony I rode, whether or not we cantered or jumped, and give myself marks out of 10. Although I loved the ponies I rode and went to bed thinking about them, trying to remember how they smelled, I never really noticed that much about them, or wondered how they felt; I suppose I was just being a child, but now it seems as though I was blind. I wonder now what happened to all those long-suffering riding-school ponies, who just put up with their lot and never complained. Looking back, I feel so sorry for them: the only time they were let out of their stables was when they were ridden in class, hour after hour spent endlessly, monotonously going round and round in circles, children tugging on their mouths and banging on their sides.

I wanted a pony of my own, desperately. Sometimes, when I took the family Labrador, Pompey, for a walk, I would carry a long twig and canter along, slapping myself on the thigh every so often; sometimes I would straddle the poor dog and try to ride him; he would sit down in protest and refuse to go on. Every birthday and Christmas morning I would look out my bedroom window and hope against hope there would be a pony, a chestnut with a white blaze, or maybe a palomino, standing on the lawn, munching. But there never was. The closest I got to owning a pony was a grey rocking horse with a red velvet saddle that I named Silver.

Just because I had riding lessons didn't mean my family had any money. I was always mortified that the only bit of proper 'kit' I owned was a pair of second-hand cord jodhpurs made many decades before Lycra was invented, and a velvet hard hat that was so precious I kept it enveloped in plastic all week; unwrapping it every Saturday morning became part of a delicious ritual. I always rode in plimsolls (my parents couldn't afford jodhpur boots), which made the other horsey girls snigger, and prompted one instructor to ask me, 'What on earth are your parents thinking? Those shoes are so dangerous. You could get trodden on, or your foot could become caught in the stirrup!' Even as a child, doing what I loved, I could never get the details quite right. I was never nonchalant. I never belonged.

I don't know why I had posters on my wall of horses rather than pop stars – I once lined my bedroom, including the door, with the front covers of *Horse and Hound*. I loved the way horses smelled. I loved the creak of a saddle when you shifted in it. I was so desperate for a pony I would force my pink-eyed white rabbit, Penny, to show jump over piles of pony paperbacks; I blamed myself when she later died of a heart attack. I would sit on my bedroom floor for hours with a tiny plastic herd, moving first one pony and then another into a field, before shutting them all in their stables for the night.

But then I grew up. I went to live in London and got a job. I didn't really think about horses, let alone dream about them, until one weekend when, only recently married, and aged about 40 (I've lied about my age so many times I have a hard time keeping track), I went on a mini-break to the Cotswolds with my husband and my passionate love affair was lit up again, like a flare (not with him, don't be silly; with horses). We were staying in a blond stone Georgian hotel. It was some dreadful time of year, like March, and outside it was so wet and windy all we did was sit in our room, trying to choose a pillow from the pillow menu. It was about five months after we'd got married and I had thought we would spend the weekend having sex, but we didn't – the only thing my husband ravaged was the mini-bar. I don't think we had sex once that entire weekend. Even on honeymoon, we only did it once. I remember thinking, as my husband heaved off of me, saying cheerfully, 'Well, you can't file for an annulment now!', that something wasn't quite right. And now here we were in the Cotswolds, in yet another lovely room, it was Saturday afternoon, and we had exhausted the amount of fun we could have by moving around and watching the Bang & Olufsen TV swivel patiently towards us.

And so we (well, I) booked to go riding at a local stables – I say local; we took two hours to find it, which of course was my fault for not plotting a course with a compass first. We got out of the car. It was still raining. I saw lots of teenage girls milling about, pushing wheelbarrows and sweeping and I thought, oh god, teenage girls still do this. How incredibly comforting they aren't all binge-vomiting down slippy sparkly vest tops. And then I walked up to the horse I had been assigned to ride, a little bay mare with a jaunty expression, sank my nose into her neck and suddenly that smell hit me. It was heady, hot horse. It felt like Saturday morning again when I was a child. I was young. I had yet to be disappointed. I was (sort of) happy.

It wasn't the best ride I've ever had: the mare was snatchy, pulling me forward out of the saddle every five seconds. I swivelled round to see my husband who was slumped like a sack of potatoes on a great big horse, giving me the look that I knew meant he blamed me for his misery. It was a look I would see often over the next few years. Cruelly, I hadn't bothered to tell him about the rising trot, so he was going bump, bump, bump right on his manhood. He was still annoyed that, as he'd clambered on board his gelding and asked the girl holding the bridle whether or not his horse 'had had children', we'd all fallen about laughing. I didn't care that I would get the silent treatment over dinner that night. I had fallen back in love with horses.

It took me a while to do something about it. For a few years, late at night, I would look at horses secretively on websites, as if I were watching porn. As well as scrolling through country houses on Primelocation.com, book-marking huge piles with land and stables, checking to see they weren't near an A road, I would visit a site called Project Horses, where difficult or unwanted or rescued horses were advertised for sale or on loan. I would look at a picture of a horse (my favourite category was 15 hands to 16.2), read about its history and its problems, and imagine my life if I owned it. Then, about two months before that fateful holiday in Africa, I stumbled upon the picture of a horse called Lizzie. She was 15.3 hands, six years old, and a former racehorse. She had been found abandoned in a field, where she had been living for some time without extra food, rugs or care. Her feet had not been trimmed and were split all the way up to her coronet band (the circle where hoof meets fur). I looked at her face, with her wide-set eyes, her huge, pricked, furry ears: she looked like a teddy. I knew, even though I lived in the middle of London and had a full-time job in an office, not to mention a full-time hobby monitoring my husband's every move, that we were meant for each other.

There is something about racehorses. They are at once so brave and fast, and so fragile. I love their faces: the extended nostrils lined with pink; the big, brown eyes; the feet like shells. I once went to watch the Grand National when I was young and although it was thrilling to see the horses thunder by in a blur – this was the Seventies, when the race was barbaric, with horses piled up, one on top of the other, flailing, hurt, soon to be shot behind a cheerful awning – I much preferred to stand beside the collecting ring, watching them being walked round by their grooms, not an ounce of fat on them, shiny as a mahogany sideboard, with perfect, Pantene manes and tails and geometric patterns on their rumps. As I got older, I realised how cruel this race, any race, can be for the horses. Flat racers are backed at two years old, which is far too young for their yet unformed skeleton; the concussion stores up terrible problems for their old age – if they ever reach old age, that is. According to Racehorse Deathwatch on the Animal Aid website, an average of 420 horses are raced to death in the UK every year. Thousands of racehorses simply disappear each year; the very few rescue charities are able to save only a handful. Steeplechasers, those that jump, are raced too often until they are too old or too tired, resulting in mistakes, broken legs, broken hearts – literally. Hallo Dandy, which won the Grand National in 1984, was found years later, abandoned and broken down, filthy and starving in a field, covered in sores.

The racing industry creates thousands upon thousands of foals each year. Out of those foals, only a few can ever be fast enough for the track. The rest have to be disposed of. Once the horse has finished racing, usually at a very young age, it's either retired, put out to stud or disposed of. Most horses don't make it to stud, as they aren't fast enough, have good enough conformation or have the pedigree. An extremely low number of racehorses are comfortably retired. That leaves the rest of the horses, about 90 per cent, to be sold, slaughtered or disposed of in another way. When there are so many horses that are being tossed aside, I often wonder why there are no laws about indiscriminate breeding in this country. I have a friend, a really stupid woman and actually not a friend at all who when I asked her why on earth she had put her not particularly well formed, bad-tempered mare in foal replied indignantly, 'She wants to be a mother.'

I emailed the woman who had rescued Lizzie, but could not afford to keep her, and arranged to go and see her the following Saturday afternoon. As I left my house, my husband was still in bed. I recognise now that he was depressed; at the time I'd just thought he was lazy. I told him I was going to see my mum. I was so excited as I drove to Hertfordshire: for the first time in years I was doing something that was all about me, not him. I knew I was acting crazily, impulsively, but I couldn't stop myself. I felt guilty, as if I were going to meet a new lover, which in a way I was.

I parked in the yard, and the woman told me the horse was still in the field. I wondered why she hadn't brought her in, spruced her up a bit, but then put that thought to one side; horsey people have the ability, always, to make me feel incompetent and foolish. It was as if I had turned up in those non-stretch jodhpurs and plimsolls all over again. She told me the mare's history or, at least, the history she knew about: she had been sold at auction at Tattersalls 'through no fault of her own', and then it was a great big blank. I studied her passport issued by Weatherbys, and only designed to help the government monitor disease; if it was meant to have protected her, it had failed miserably. Her racing name is What A Carve Up. Her dam is Pussy-Puss-Willow, her sire Carve His Name in Pride. When I got home I looked up her father on the internet. He is still at stud in Devon, and is now over 20 years old, having produced numerous National Hunt winners and several top three-day eventers. What went wrong? Potentially Lizzie must have been worth thousands, if not hundreds of thousands, and yet here she was with broken feet, filthy and neglected in a field.

We walked over to her. She immediately put her head straight up, like a llama, and galloped towards us. It was as if she had been waiting for me. She nuzzled my trousers, and I gave her the organic M&S carrot batons I had brought with me. I circled her slowly, letting her know where I was by keeping a hand on her flank, and I could see she was in a terrible state: very thin and ribby, with a staring coat, and hooves that looked so painful I wondered how she could even walk on them. I buried my nose in her neck and she jumped, startled, unused to affection, not sure how to deal with it. 'We think she has been beaten up by a man, mistreated and then tossed aside because they couldn't handle her,' said the woman. Reluctantly, I walked away, climbed over the gate and looked back at her, standing knee-deep in mud in that cold, windy, rutted field. She wickered to me. I told her I'd be back to fetch her soon.

When I got home, I didn't tell my husband what had happened. He asked after my mum, and I said she was fine. When he'd gone to bed, I sat at my laptop and emailed the woman to tell her I would buy Lizzie. I told her I had nowhere to keep her at the moment, but that I would find somewhere and contact her when I got back from holiday: we were about to take that ill-fated, many-planed trip to Vamizi. Looking back, maybe I pushed my husband too far on that holiday, made him confess to me, evicted him from the island and filed for divorce because I knew I would be coming home to Lizzie, and that he would have disapproved, laughed at me, told me I was ridiculous. Maybe it was fate, I don't know. But having to get myself organised for my new horse and my new life kept me sane during those first few weeks on my own. After much searching and phoning, I found a livery yard on the edge of Windsor Great Park. I knew that I wanted my horse to live with me, that I wanted to be able to look out my bedroom window and see her, standing there, munching, but it was going to take a while. This would be a good stopgap while I put my house on the market and found somewhere for us both to live.

And so two weeks later I was stood in flip-flops (I still didn't have a pair of wretched riding boots), waiting for the lorry to turn up. I heard her before I saw her. A horrible, high-pitched screaming. As the lorry turned into the drive I could hear her hooves, smashing into the back of the box. The woman driving the lorry looked pale. She parked and we lowered the ramp. Lizzie swung her head round, wild eyes swivelling. Her whole body was heaving and steaming. With a front foot she pawed the floor, furious, impatient. I wanted to unload my own horse, to walk her out quietly into her new home, but the woman stopped me. She untied the rope and Lizzie just spun round, almost falling down the ramp backwards. Eventually, with her spinning around, me holding determinedly onto a piece of rope with a horse dancing on the other end like a malevolent balloon, we got her into her loose box, with its deep bed of shavings, full hay net and bucket of water.

The woman handed me a bottle of black liquid. 'This is what we gave her to calm her down,' she said. 'I'd carry on with it for a bit if I were you.' She took off Lizzie's headcollar. 'Aren't you leaving that?' I asked her, realising I didn't yet have one. 'Sorry,' she said, and was gone.

For two hours I watched my horse in her stable, circling

endlessly, grabbing a mouthful of hay and then spitting it out over the door. She would frequently swing her head at her sides, biting her own shoulders. Goodness, I thought, I didn't know that horses self-harm. Every now and then she would kick the wall, violently, leaving great big holes. At one point I opened the door to pour more water into her bucket and she pounced at me with both front feet, teeth bared, like a giant kitten. No wonder she had been abandoned in a field. No wonder the woman hadn't brought her in when she showed her to me. 'Got your hands full there,' said the owner of the yard, a hard sort with a red face and Thelwell behind who had probably been born wearing breeches. I knew that Lizzie was terrified. I was terrified. She had nothing. I had nothing. I switched off her light and reluctantly drove home to my lovely, warm, empty house, wondering what on earth I'd taken on.

CHAPTER 6

* * *

(In which I wonder, where is bleeding Hugh Fearnley-Whittingstall when you need him?)

The number of times I've shrieked because of low-flying bats: about a million.

The number of visitors to my wild bird-feeding stations: none. What are they waiting for?

The number of times I've seen a toadstool and thought, hmm, I wonder if that's a mushroom, and vice versa. About four million.

Let me take you on a tour of my farm. As you leave the porch at the back of the house you walk through lavender beds that have gone a bit leggy to a rose-strewn arch in an iron-railings fence, which is rusty and falling down but reminds me of the parkland at Babington House, or the approach to the house at the beginning of the film *Atonement*. You then walk down some crumbling stone steps into the top paddock, which is ringed with copper beech and sycamore. To the right is the orchard, and beyond that another small field that once housed the vegetable garden: there is now a gate leading into a walled enclosure of nettles. Left is another orchard with about four trees, all of which are covered in moss and in the Gloria Hunniford stage of their lives, and a small pond surrounded by forget-me-nots; a lot of toads live here, and tiny water voles – at least, I think that's what they are; they might just be mice that like to cool off, or fancy themselves as mini Michael Phelpses.

Straight down the hill, through the rickety old gate held together with baling twine (it reminds me of me), is the 26-acre field, otherwise known as 'the big field': in summer it's dotted with harebells. The bottom of the hill is boggy: there are always a lot of mushrooms, although of course they might be toadstools – where is Hugh Fearnley-Whittingstall when you need him? You go left, over a stream that's always in a rush, and into the 20-acre field, with a hill just like the one in *Teletubbies*, and an eight-acre wood. This is 'the hill field' flanked by the stream that flows into a lake, my lake, with a tiny wooden jetty complete with deflated rubber ring, bulrushes and a proprietorial kingfisher with an oversize, positively Cyrano de Bergerac beak and outfit by Christian Lacroix. A pair of grey heron lives on the lake, a gangly couple that take flight whenever they see me. You walk in a great big curve, up through the square field (square and flat), and through the Quality Street paddock (it's green and triangular) and round to the front of the house. All the fields are surrounded by dense, ancient hedgerows several feet thick that in spring are littered with bright green ferns and purple foxgloves: I love the little dots in the flowers that show the bees which way to go should they become confused, drunk on nectar.

The garden, which surrounds the house on three sides, is beautiful, if wild and unkempt: full of lupins, golden rod, hollyhocks, rhododendron bushes and, how apt, the hot-pink rods of Love-Lies-Bleeding. There's a pear tree climbing up one corner of the house, reaching right up to the windows of what is now my bedroom; unfortunately, I don't like pears. There are lots of smells, textures and sounds I'd completely forgotten from my childhood: the grey fur on lupin-seed pods, the Lancaster bomber drone of bumble bees, the dense Christmas lantern effect of dahlias, the throaty call of wood pigeons, the scent of rhubarb, the subtle taste of blackberries.

The early Victorian farmhouse is deceptively rather lovely from the outside (it's also warmer outside than in; I'm beginning to wonder whether or not it's haunted) with its porches and verandah of cobblestones. It overlooks the original, untouched for decades (apart from someone nicking the weathervane) stable block, the reason I wanted the house the moment I saw it. As well as the four loose boxes, there's a tack room with a cobbled floor and a hay barn with beautiful, lofty pale oak rafters. On second thoughts, I might just live in the barn instead of the house. It really is more me.

What really sold me on the house and land, though, apart from its possibility as a racehorse and cat spa, and its 46 acres of pasture and eight acres of woods (so many grand houses are stood, cuckoo-chick like, in just an acre or two of land; I saw a William and Mary house a few miles outside Bath, but it had only a lovely garden and small paddock that Lizzie would have churned to mud in an instant), was its location slap-bang in the middle of Exmoor National Park, almost 300 square miles of time-warp Britain, home of Lorna Doone and Evelyn Waugh (his family home, Pixton Park House, is only half a mile from my farm) and, now, me. It's as if, once you cross its borders, you've been transported in a Tardis all the way back to the 1930s: there are rickety signposts that still point the way to long-closed railway stations. There are no supermarkets, few petrol stations, no cashpoints, no endless roundabouts. The moorland itself is beautiful: purple in summer, white in winter. The grass is cropped short, like velvet, by sheep, wild ponies and a particularly hairy brand – breed, sorry; I still have my fashion hat on – of cattle. On the hills, such as the Harrison Ford-sounding Dunkery Beacon and the Valley of the Stones, where Percy Shelley once wandered, are wild goats, nosy, sure-footed creatures built on springs who chew with their mouths open, while up above all manner of birds of prey – kite, kestrel, peregrine falcon (these have speckly trousers, like an owl's) – circle on warm currents of air, the tips of their wings tilted upwards, like EasyJets. There are big, ghostly barn owls that sit in the middle of the road, bold as brass, making you swerve around them before they lift heavily, laboriously, into the air. When I wake up early, and look out to the east, I can see a herd of 30 or 40 red deer, all straight out of Disney central casting.

I had been to the West Country before, but had never set foot on Exmoor until I went to look at my farm, having spotted it on Primelocation.com. Every summer, my parents would take their seven ungrateful children for a week in a rented flat in a Victorian pile called 'Willoughby' overlooking the genteel regency seaside town of Sidmouth. I recently went back for the day because I had wanted Michael the sheepdog to dip his paw in the sea, and had been thwarted by the 'no dogs' signs that now police our coastlines – what about a sign saying 'no children'? – and was stunned to see a Bath Stone beauty called Peak House on the slopes overlooking Jacob's Ladder. I'd never noticed it during those long days huddled on the beach in loons and too-tight cheesecloth shirt (my dad, though, always walked around with his shirt off, exposing a Cary Grant tan despite the inclement weather. 'At least we all had a good blow,' my mum would say cheerfully). But Peak House must have been there: it was built in the 18th century; despite what my ex-husband would have you believe. I'm not quite that old, so why hadn't I even seen it? The M4 and M5 were only partially open so the trip in our overcrowded Hillman Minx took the best part of a day. Remember the scene where the American arrives at Fawlty Towers, tired, cross, hungry and demanding? That was us. I wonder now why on earth, instead of making us spend each day sat on towels on the damp red sand, eating buttered rolls and getting colder and more windswept, my parents didn't take us walking on Dartmoor or Exmoor with a pair of binoculars and a guide book. But I suppose we would have complained about doing that, too.

As a child, I had no interest in wildlife; I was firmly

focused on pets. Growing up in semi-rural Essex, I paid no heed to what was outside my window. Then, the countryside meant long waits in dirty, vandalised bus shelters. It meant rabbits dying messily, sightlessly, from myxomatosis. It meant barbed wire and stubble and bullocks and bypasses. I might have gone riding, but I never went on hacks, just round and round on a rectangle of sawdust, occasionally performing a figure of eight or a serpentine loop. But Exmoor? Well, this is proper countryside. A wilderness. It has impenetrable fogs. If you go for a walk, you need sensible boots, a waterproof coat and a compass. Best of all, it's totally uncommutable from London. And with its hundreds of miles of bridle paths it's a paradise for someone who suddenly finds themselves the owner of an unrehabilitated (I hate that term; it's as though she is in prison for burglary and having to learn how to operate a trouser press or sew mailbags) 15 hands 3 inches high racehorse.

CHAPTER 7

* * *

(In which my racehorse thinks she is a giraffe)

I have precisely one week from moving in to get everything ready for Lizzie. I make a list. I'm good at lists. I suppose the one below is my equivalent to be being broody and ordering changing mats and Eeyore-covered organic sleepsuits from John Lewis ...

- Wheelbarrow
- Hay fork and shovel
- Broom
- Non-slip rubber mats for stable floors
- Four hay bars (hay nets, which force the horse into an unnatural feeding position, and place pressure on the jaw, are so last season)
- Rubber feed bowls and water buckets
- A hose pipe
- Saddle brackets and bridle hooks
- Saddle and bridle, stirrups, girth, headcollar, numnah and lead rope (the last two both in black as she needs to co-ordinate with Mummy)
- Lunge rope

- Brushing boots (these go around her tendons while being exercised to avoid injury)
- Overreach boots (these go around her front feet, in case she treads on herself with her rear feet)
- Knee boots (in case she trips on the road; we don't, like poor old Ginger, want broken knees)
- Circingle (this goes around her waist, like a cummerbund; don't ask me why or what it's for)
- Grooming kit: dandy brush, body brush, curry comb (it cleans the body brush), mane comb, hoof pick, sponge (one for eyes and nostrils, one for the dock – bottom – area)
- Hoof oil
- Four rugs, one each for day, night, turnout and sweat
- Summer sheet in blue check
- Feed scoop, two
- Organic wild birdseed and four birdfeeders. These prove to be the best investment I've ever made in my life. Watching the blue tits, great tits, a bullfinch with his rose-coloured breast and white rump, a green woodpecker who wears a jaunty red scarf, a jay with his blush-pink vest and the treecreeper each day on the red maple outside my office window is like having a front-row seat at the Cirque du Soleil. There are also lots of house sparrows, solving the mystery of why they disappeared from London: obviously they all wanted to downsize. I've made particular friends with a married pair of collared doves, a robin whom I call, rather unimaginatively, Robin, and a male pheasant who has taken refuge in my garden from the Somme-like guns

that face him out on the moor. When Snoopy spotted him for the first time – he was the first to brave the cat flap; it was like seeing my only son go over the top – his eyes were as large as dinner plates

- A hard hat (oh that my mum didn't have dementia so that I could ask her what on earth happened to my old one so that I could save some money)
- A back protector (these hadn't been invented when I was a child. In retrospect, I could've been killed. Oh, happy release)
- Hay, straw, feed

Um, what do horses eat these days, I wonder to myself as I sit in bed (the removal men finally arrived, having had the brainwave to decant all my stuff into a fleet of smaller vans), wearing three pairs of socks, a Burberry beanie, fingerless gloves and a hot-water bottle strapped to my tummy in case I have to go to the loo in the middle of the night. I grab a torch, kindly given to me by one of the removal men in exchange for not telling him off for scratching my plasma television, and pad downstairs to the great big boxes still unopened in my office with its walls scribbled on by generations of bored rural children in the brief window before they discovered solvents, and delve into the one marked 'horse'. I dig out my *Manual of Horsemanship*, published in 1950; my mum bought it for me in a jumble sale when I was nine. I flick through it. I see the section entitled 'How to make a wisp, with diagrams'; it's as if I'd read it yesterday. I never did get round to making one of those. Hmm, let's see. Oats, cubes, barley, maize, wheat, bran, bran mash. I flick to the section entitled 'How to Groom': 'In the morning, put the headcollar on the horse. Tie him on a short rack [?], and remove his rugs. If cold, leave one blanket folded over his loins. It's often more pleasant in summer to go outside [the author obviously never lived in Somerset]. Begin by picking out the hooves, working downwards from the heel towards the toe. When picking out the feet, it's permissible to lift the off feet from the near side. Quartering is done first thing in the morning, to remove stable stains. The object is to make the horse look tidy before exercise. The eyes, nostrils and dock are sponged. Particular attention should be paid to the removal from the flanks of stains. In the evening, the horse is set fair, given a light brush over and wisping when the rugs are being changed, droppings removed and bedding tidied up. To prevent littering of the yard, feet should be picked out several times a day.'

There is nothing on what to do if your horse refuses to pick up her feet or, when you enter the stable to put on her headcollar, sticks her head in the air like a giraffe, turns her rump on you, and hides in a corner. Ah well.

In the two weeks before moving to Exmoor, I had screaming matches down the phone with my soon-to-be-ex-husband. During London Fashion Week, he had yelled, 'Why should I just walk away from the house?' 'Do whatever you think is morally right,' was my calm, cool reply. In between the arguments I had found out the name of the local farrier, who turned out to be more booked up than Madonna's plastic surgeon, and the name of the local equine vet. I had also acquired another horse – a pony, to be precise, called Benji. When I told the livery in Windsor that I was moving Lizzie to Exmoor, the hard woman in breeches with the Thelwell bottom actually laughed, which I suppose was warranted as I could barely get Lizzie out of her box and into the paddock for her requisite two hours of freedom a day. I was worried about Lizzie being on her own and so I contacted an organisation called Intelligent Horsemanship. They told me of a pony who, unless he found a new owner, was going to be shot at the end of the week. He had started to buck off any child who clambered onto his back, but as long as he was never ridden again, he was perfect and could act as Lizzie's chaperone. They said he was a bright bay, with a handsome face, and 14 hands 2 in; just the pony I'd dreamed about when I was 12. I phoned his owner and learned that, apart from his back problem, he was in fine fettle. I arranged for the horsebox to pick him up on the way down from Windsor with Lizzie, sight unseen. She would be on a sort of horsey speed date.

And so, on a dark, cold Saturday evening at the beginning of November, I'm standing in the lane with a torch, waiting for Benji and Lizzie. The rubber matting has been laid and the straw beds have been made. I've soaked their feeds and filled their water buckets. The hay bars are full to the brim; to my shame, I found that, despite 20 years of aerobics classes, I still can't lift a bale of hay. I had pictured, dreamed about the moment I would walk my very own horse into my very own yard since I was five years old and I am, incredibly, about to do it for real. This beats walking down the bloody aisle. There's something about walking alongside a beautiful horse with pricked ears that is magical, special. I'm so excited I can barely wait any longer and then I spot the headlights. They are here.

It's 2 am, and I'm exhausted. Lizzie and Benji arrived and, although both were fine, not sweaty or bothered at all by the five-hour journey, I was annoyed no one had thought to put on the bandages I had provided to protect their legs and tails. Lizzie came off first – I noticed she appeared to have conjunctivitis in both eyes, probably from the livery's habit of simply tossing hay over her door – and she led me without incident into her box, squeezing me out the way so that she could go first. Then came Benji: he rushed off the ramp, all pleased and keen, blissfully unaware how close he had come to being sent to an abattoir. I put him next to Lizzie, who immediately stuck her head over the partition to see what he was doing. I gave them both a feed, garnished with sliced Cox's apples and hand-picked pears. I stood watching them eat and then I noticed that Benji's neck was covered in sweat. I unbolted his door and ran my hands over his body. His belly was sopping wet, too. I called his owner, the woman who had placed so little value on his life, unconcerned that his reward for teaching so many dreadful children to ride was to have him sent, like the carthorse in Orwell's *Animal Farm* (the TV animation of the book haunts me still), to be made into glue. 'He might have caught a chill in the trailer,' she said. 'Or are the lights in the stable too bright? He might be really hot.'

What does she think I'm running, a solarium? I stood there, watching Benji. Lizzie had her head permanently over the partition wall, watching him, anxious but still chewing. Two hours later he was dripping with sweat and coughing violently. His legs started to buckle, his head swayed, and he looked as though he was about to go down. I put his headcollar on and tried to hold him up, all one and a half tons of him. This is ridiculous, I said to myself. I've only had him a few hours and he's about to die. I called his owner again. Her mobile was now switched off. And so I called the vet. They agreed to send someone out immediately. Benji kept coughing and I started to cry, feeling like that girl in unsuitable plimsolls all over again, the one who cannot do anything right. Who takes on too much. Who's always doing things that scare her.

The vet, Simon, was sympathetic. He listened to Benji's heart and chest, and told me he has asthma (Benji, not the vet, who seemed perfectly fine, if rather posh). He gave him an injection to help his breathing, and handed me an inhaler, an ordinary, human asthma inhaler, which I must puff 10 times into his mouth, twice a day. Easier said than done, it would turn out. I asked Simon what on earth I had been doing wrong, that 'Maybe it's my 1950 *Manual of Horsemanship*?', and he laughed. 'When someone wants to get rid of a pony, they often won't tell you what's wrong with it. This is a longstanding problem. Benji shouldn't really be in a stable, on all this straw, eating hay. That's probably what set him off. And when you turn him out, he can't really be on 46 acres. He needs to be in a small paddock, with restricted grazing, otherwise he will get laminitis.' I later look laminitis up in my manual; similar to gout, it can be fatal, occurs in ponies and is caused by overfeeding.

And so it turns out I have a pony who's allergic to being a pony. His treatment over the coming months would cost £4,000. I had had him insured, but as he fell ill within the first 14 days of my owning him – it was within the first 14 minutes, actually – I turned out not to be covered at all. He cannot live in a stable, and Lizzie, being a thin-skinned flibbertigibbet thoroughbred, cannot live out at night in the winter. She needs lots of lush grass to fatten her up, while Benji needs a square of scrub. Rather than being companions, they are to conduct a long-distance relationship with very different interests and hobbies. Which is hard, given that the next morning, having dragged myself out of bed (I soon learn to save time in the mornings by wearing my jodhpurs, jumper and socks to bed; however, the cats don't budge all day from their teapot positions on my cashmere bed linen from Mint on Wigmore Street) to feed them at 8 am, I lead Benji out to the top paddock while Lizzie, still in her stable, cannot believe her eyes that he has left her even momentarily. 'Chill out,' I tell her. 'At least he's not having sex with a 37-year-old trollop he met on holiday who lives in New York.' She begins to bang on her door, heaving her weight against it so that it bows, ominously: the horse equivalent, I suppose, of texting him to ask what time he'll be home for dinner. She circles, endlessly, whinnying plaintively.

I go back to fetch her, open the stable door and she pushes past me, eyes only for her beloved, rather like a pubescent girl at a David Cassidy concert. One day in, on chapter one of the story entitled *Liz Has Two Ponies*, I already have a seemingly insurmountable problem. That night I go to bed and, in the middle of the night, am woken by a high-pitched cry from Susie. I sit up. Something runs towards me, and I realise with a screech that it's a mouse. It hides beneath Squeaky's tummy; she is lying in her usual place in my right armpit. She barely gives it a glance before it runs out again, straight into the jaws of Snoopy, who clamps his jaws around its neck before all four little pink legs stop bicycling. Honestly, it's carnage. Carnage.

CHAPTER 8

* * *

(In which I find I'm living in the High Chaparral, without Blue and Manolo, unfortunately)

It's late November. It gets so dark so early, I might as well be living in Norway. I get a phone call. It's my solicitor. She tells me my decree absolute has come through, along with what she calls a 'clean break'. This means neither me nor my husband has any rights to one another's past or future earnings. But it all seems a bit dirty to me. He has kept up the wounded party stance, wondering why he had been decanted into a basement bedsit (hovel) while I stayed in the family home (I figured: I paid for everything, he bought an oven glove), while I can't help wondering why on earth he married me in the first place. Why didn't he just say, 'Listen, Lizzie, I'm 28, I need to live a little, sow a few wild oats, move out of my mum's and grow up a bit and learn to fend for myself before settling down. Why don't you just keep the £20,000 you were going to spend on our wedding at Babington House and get a face lift?'

He was sleeping with other women so soon into our marriage (I'm still receiving emails from women telling me he had tried to get them into bed – 'Let me be your Christmas cracker' had been one of his chat-up lines; this was to the yoga instructor. I imagine her to have unwashed hair and a yeast infection) that upon hearing the divorce is final, that I'm no longer married, that when flying to the US I will for evermore have to put 'none' in the box asking how many family members are travelling with me, to be honest I don't feel any different at all. I don't even feel relieved. I just feel nothing. My main memory of the marriage is going to M&S in my lunch hour, spending a million pounds on food and getting carrier bag fingers.

I decide to get some chickens. I don't particularly like eggs, but I figure the former battery hens from a rescue centre in Devon deserve their retirement, to get off the treadmill, to have their own personal space at last, beholden to no one (a little like me, etc). I've also read somewhere that they eat tics, something my cats are currently plagued with; I live in fear of Lyme disease although perhaps this is something you only get in the Deep South.

Having picked the chickens up and found they weigh less than a feather, which is ironic, seeing as they have so few, the rest having been brutally pecked from them (their bottoms look as though they have just had a very inexpert Brazilian), I placed them in cat baskets in the back of my BMW. 'Oooh,' they squawked, looking round them, 'We've gone up in the world!' I misguidedly install them with straw and perches, which they are too weak to climb onto (they gaze at the contraptions much as I once gazed at the rope in PE class) in a large stone outhouse in the

Gloria Hunniford orchard. They huddle together, trying to pool the few feathers they have between them. When I return in the dead of night to check on them, seated at the grain in their Conran Shop bowl are three large rats, tucking in. I wouldn't have been surprised to see the rats with white napkins around their necks, so at home do they appear. They don't even budge when they see me, they merely return to their feast. The chickens are scrunched in one corner, looking terrified, as if to say, 'Even when we were in battery cages, we didn't have to share our dinner with rats.' I realise I must move them tomorrow, into the house if needs be.

I'm starting to think that Lizzie might be schizophrenic. When I emerge from the porch in the morning, hopping on one leg, trying to put my Hunter wellies on, she whinnies to me and nods her head like Champion the Wonder Horse. I go into the tack room to mix her and Benji's feed. I put hers in a box at her feet, then tramp across the yard to where Benji is standing miserably in the field, doing his broken-down carthorse stance. 'If only,' I can hear him thinking as he waits in vain for Lizzie to join him in her negligee, 'I had internet porn.' I then fetch Lizzie's headcollar. Once she has finished eating (she hates me watching, flattening her huge ears, waggling her nose), I enter her stable to begin the ritual of chasing her round and round the box, trying to put it over her nose; you would think I was trying to murder her. I've discovered that if I lasso her neck with the lead rope, I can then control her sufficiently to get the halter on. Once that's done, I undo her rug, slide it off, inhaling the hot, sweet smell of horse and, depending on the weather, either leave her naked or put her outdoor rug on. She wears a bright blue Lycra T-shirt over her chest to stop the rug rubbing on her delicate skin; she reminds me of an Eighties aerobics teacher. I then open the door and she barges past me, head up, tail in a question mark, towards Benji, who gives her a sharp nip before they both bugger off for the day. She's still without shoes as her feet look split and sore and misshapen. I find the name of a company called Trinity Consultants on the internet, and phone a remarkably knowledgeable man called Roger to ask for his advice. I tell him my horse seems to be very anxious, hates to be left alone, and has badly neglected feet; in a few months, this would perfectly describe me. He prescribes a supplement containing magnesium for her moods called Attitude Adjuster Two, and a special potion to promote healthy hoof growth.

However, I reckon that her feet need trimming to prevent the cracks splaying further, and so I call the farrier. He arrives three hours late. I discover that, just like her mummy, Lizzie isn't particularly trustful of men. Her ears go back, her eyes swivel, and it's all I can do to hold her head while the farrier gets his anvil and pliers out of the van. He picks up her near fore. I notice he doesn't talk to her first, let her smell him or even stroke her. I tell him I think that shoulder is sore because she is very defensive if you touch her there or even attempt to use a body brush on her. He doesn't answer. Perhaps he is deaf, or I'm invisible. He picks up her foot, something I've so far failed to do. Like lightning, and before I can stop her, she swings her head and bites him, hard, on his bald patch. There is a lot of blood. He stands up, staggering, and as he does so he punches her in the stomach. I can't believe that he hit my horse. I tell him to put his tools down and to back away from my horse. 'Why didn't you try to get to know her first or even ask me about her? I'm not asking you to trim her hooves as a favour, I'm paying you for your time,' I say to him, but he is already back in his van, not even bothering to ask for his money. 'I'm so sorry, Lizzie,' I say as we dance back to the field. 'I will never let a man near you or me again. That's a cast-iron promise.'

I've been worrying about leaving Benji in the field at night on his own when fortune drops the solution into my lap, or at least my inbox. A woman has emailed me a picture of her New Forest pony, Dream, who desperately needs a new home. She bought her for her daughter, but she was so naughty (the pony, not the daughter) she put her out on loan to people who forgot that Dream, given the chance, tends to eat all her bedding. Having consumed several square metres of straw, Dream contracted colic, a dangerous form of constipation where the gut can twist, and promptly fell over, breaking her pelvis. She had to stand on a box rest for months while the joints mended, but now, well, she is crippled. She has developed an extraordinary crab-like gait, and her belly swings very low. It was the picture that sold me on her, though. She was flying through the air, Farrah Fawcett mane lifting in the wind, full of joy. I thought she would make the perfect companion for Benji the companion. I wish I had known as a child, yearning for my very own pony, how disposable they really are, how unwanted, how cheap, and not treasured at all.

When her owner drops her off the following week, Benji and Lizzie are looking over the gate, nosy as ever, wondering who on earth is coming to see them. Dream whickers. Benji answers. It's love at first sight. Now all I need is another companion for Lizzie. I seem to be well on the way to having my very own herd. Sometimes, what with all the whinnying and stampeding when they hear the postman, it's like living in the High Chaparral only without Manolo and Blue (without any men at all, actually). I sometimes look at Lizzie, with her fear of headcollars and picking her feet up, and wonder how on earth cowboys ever managed to be quite so cavalier (isn't it interesting that a word so integrated with horses now means something so casual), slinging on saddles that must have weighed a ton, leaping onto horses without so much as a by your leave. I don't yet have an outdoor school for Lizzie, but yesterday I took her into the top paddock on a long rope and gently placed a circingle around her tummy, a prelude to putting a saddle and girth on so she would get to know how it feels, a little like trying on her first bra. I took a few steps back and encouraged her to walk in a circle around me. She literally went up in the air, all four feet off the ground, back arched like a bronco. Oh dear, I thought. It looked so easy when Robert Redford did it. I might have been rather optimistic in booking the fitter from Balance Saddles: a holistic and kind method of saddling, with a very wide tree that allows the horse's back to be rounded rather than squeezed into the more habitual shape of a shark's fin. I might have to postpone it a bit.

I think my standards of grooming are slipping, and not just according to my manual of horsemanship. This is what is happening to my body as I race headlong towards 50. I have a wide stripe of grey hair in my parting, mainly due to the fact I don't have time to drive the 40 miles to the nearest hairdresser; in London I would go every two weeks, without fail, to my vegetable colourist at the Aveda salon. I'm worried I now so closely resemble a badger a passing farmer might gas me. My legs are covered in thick black hair with a lampshade fringe at my ankles; I figure at least it's extra insulation. I don't think they have much truck with the Hollywood wax this far out of London: on the rural disapproval rating I think it's up there with stilettos and clean cream leather interiors of cars and central heating. I no longer possess the illuminated magnifying mirror I had in my old bathroom, so I'm sure my face is sprouting all sorts of unspeakable things. It never ceases to amaze me that while the hairs on my eyebrows never recovered from the shock of an over-zealous plucking in the Seventies performed so that at least one part of me would resemble the model in the Sarah Moon Biba poster, the hairs on my chin are of positively Brooke Shields-worthy dimensions. The number of times I've thought: Oh dear God, is this the menopause? About 40 million. My feet, well, I never see my feet because I can't bear to take off my Selina Scott goat's wool socks. It's not good.

All of my jackets, even my Dries van Noten ones, have

green slobber on them, mainly courtesy of Benji, who has no manners. I had imagined I would wear a sort of Toast catalogue assortment of grey cashmere leggings and thick socks, all lit by firelight (did I mention that despite the fact it's a habit banned in most civilised nations, my chimney smokes, so that each night I sit there, watery-eyed?), but somehow there never seems to be enough time to get dressed properly. On one of my increasingly rare sorties into London to visit the new Westfield London shopping mall to fulfil my duties as a fashion-editor-at-large of a national newspaper, the male PR said to me, 'So, is it lovely and peaceful down there in Somerset? How are you getting on now that you've downsized?' Is it peaceful? Is it bugger. I forgot, perhaps never fully understood, that life in the countryside is not really like those serene Burberry ads where you stand around looking picturesque beneath trees. Young women don't really traipse through fields in soft tweeds from Dolce & Gabbana. Women here, even young, beautiful ones, wear thick, fleecy navy things from Primark or green nylon contraptions from gun shops. It's all an elaborate lie, fuelled by photographs of designers like Luella Bartley exercising their horses bareback on the beach at Cornwall. As we have seen, you're not even allowed to walk your dog on the beaches of the glorious south-west, let alone ride your horse.

I should have known the countryside would be like this: wet, windy and inconvenient. At the chemist – a pretty, stone affair with original cabinets in my local market town of Dulverton – I actually have to order my special toothpaste and mouthwash. I once went to the Scottish Borders to interview the aristocratic face of Burberry, Stella Tennant. She picked me up in a beaten-up old estate car with rubbish on the floor, wearing no make-up, dreadful Converse sneakers and ancient cords. Her house, which had been photographed for American *Vogue*, smelt of wet Labrador. It was freezing. She told me that she and her incredibly handsome French husband hadn't eaten out once since moving there. And I thought I could do it better, more photogenically, than she had? I must have been mad. At the moment, I wake up, hardly daring to poke my poor chapped hands outside my duvet cover, and wish with every bone in my tired old corpse to be back in my pink bedroom in that garden square, with nothing to do all day other than potter in the warm and the dry.

CHAPTER 9

* * *

(In which I turn into my ex-husband's sexless nan)

M y mobile rings. I've found that if I'm at the top of the house, in the room that I laughingly call 'the second bathroom' because it contains an old toilet I've yet to peer down and a ripped bit of wall where a sink used to be, I can get a signal. It's my ex-husband.

'Hi, Chubby. I just wanted to say Happy Christmas.'

'Are you at your mum's?'

'No, I'm in my flat [hovel] eating dry pitta bread. I was wondering if I could come and see you and Snoopy and the girls [he means Squeaky, Susie and Sweetie, not his various mistresses] on Boxing Day.'

I say yes, I suppose so. I'm already thinking of all the things I will have to do before he gets here (wax my legs, dye my hair, look at my feet, cleanse, tone, moisturise, buy food, get the house renovated, valet the car, hose the wheelie bins, groom Lizzie, both of them) and all the hoops I will have to jump through once he's arrived. I will have to assume my usual position of sympathetically cocked head as he tells me how depressed he has been, how alone, how his career's over and do I have any Brie? He tells me he will be spending Christmas Day with his family, but will indeed come down on Boxing Day. 'I'll call you when I'm on the train. What station do I have to go to? Do you know how much the ticket will cost? Shall I get a return or two singles?'

It's now Christmas Day. The house is colder than a coffin, and so having wrestled with Lizzie (we are like that cartoon, when Sylvester finally catches Sweetie Pie and it's a blur of flying fur and arms and squeals) and turned her out to join Benji and Dream, whom I now refer to as 'the honeymooners', I spend the morning carrying logs into the house, attempting in a very Buddhist manner to rehome the wood lice. I had gone into Dulverton on Christmas Eve to find all the shops had shut at 4 pm; most shut at midday on a Saturday. Only the delicatessen was open, so I crawled in, as if it were the base station on Everest. The woman behind the counter is very young and beautiful, something you don't get a lot of on Exmoor: if someone has teeth, it's a bonus. She has dark, wavy hair and is wearing pale foundation and blue glittery eyeshadow. She has on a pink V-neck sweater, scarves, and an apron – the sort of outfit you can't quite pin down but which looks marvellous.

'Hello,' she said, smiling brightly. 'My name is Emily.' Again, this is something I don't think I will ever get used to in the countryside: people, complete strangers, look you in the eye and smile and speak to you. At my Sainsbury's Local in Islington there were just rows of sullen girls in headscarves who lived in a parallel universe where you didn't exist. I told Emily I needed food because my ex-husband is coming the next day and while I had expected the countryside to be bursting with local produce, all I've been able to find in the nine weeks since moving here is a Spar with past-their-sell-by-dates new potatoes in dented tins. I didn't even know they still made such stuff. She loaded me up with coffee beans, lovely solid brown bread, pasta in a nice box, sun-dried tomatoes, Somerset cheeses including Brie, and tangerines and walnuts. A bit of an odd meal, but I'm sure it will do. She told me she used to babysit for the children who lived in my house before their parents (the thieving dirty bastards) divorced and sold it to me. 'The house is hideous, isn't it?' I said to her.

'No, it could be amazing,' she replies. 'But it's always been cold. I think that's because it stands on a hill, but at least that means you won't get flooded. The children used to sleep beneath three duvets and a Golden Retriever.' She told me her boyfriend lives in my village – I don't actually live in a village, but about two miles up the hill – and I told her they must come over for a drink while my ex-husband is down. I realised I'm segueing into old behaviour patterns: safety in numbers, deflection away from me, that sort of thing.

On Boxing Day I wake up, moderately excited. I realise I might actually be about to speak to someone who isn't stood behind a till. I break the habit of a lifetime and tint my roots myself, something my London hairdresser was always accusing me of but up until now the evidence for which had been entirely circumstantial. I shave my legs, thus destroying several decades of good work. I put on clean jodhpurs and a £500 Dolce & Gabbana sweater littered with sequins. I let the chickens out of their Christmas present: a brand-new wooden house on stilts that is completely rat-proof and has a tiny ramp that can be let down, like a drawbridge. They blink in the searing brilliance of my sequins. Even they are feeling festive. I think of bribing them at some point in the future to let me have a lie-in. My mobile goes. It's a text. 'Got to Paddington to find there are no trains on Boxing Day. Will come tomorrow. N'

Typical. When he does finally arrive at my tiny railway station a day later than expected, I can tell it's him by the fact he's last off the bridge over the track; he is even beaten by old ladies using walking frames. He's carrying a giant rucksack and when he spots me, sitting in my car looking decorative and nonchalant, he beams. He later tells me I lit up the inside of my car so brightly it was as though I had the interior light on. 'I did,' I say. 'I was reading a book waiting for you to get off the train.' We are already sparring like medieval jousters; I should just dress Benji and Lizzie up in masks and brightly covered coats and have done with it. He throws his stuff in my boot and gets in. 'Merry Christmas,' he says, giving me a dry peck, like a tortoise.

We set off beneath trees laden with so many crystals they look as though they have been decorated by Swarovski, past rivers with leaping fish and diving birds, over stone bridges above tiny brooks, even past a baby deer in the road, and he says nothing. I steal a glance at him to ask him whether he has been struck blind and simply forgotten to tell me and find he is looking down intently at his mobile. When we arrive, he throws his bags down in the hall and opens the fridge: it's tiny, sat on the floor, a temporary stopgap until I can afford to get the kitchen done up by the nice German engineers at Bulthaup. He doesn't comment. He then puts a hand in his big black bag and I think for a moment he's going to pull out a present, but it's only his laptop. He logs on. He is gone.

The next morning – he slept in the spare room; I now feel like his nan. Snoopy, rather disloyally, joined him. My heart leapt when I saw my little cat put his tiny head forward for his habitual kiss – he eventually emerges when I've done a full day's hard labour on the yard. 'Have you looked at the incredible view?' I ask him. 'Not yet.' After two days, he cautiously ventures outside for the first time, like someone leaving an igloo and worried about polar bears. I have to help him on with a pair of Wellingtons, and as I do so I feel like a mummy in a playground helping a giant toddler. He shuffles off to 'get some logs. It's bloody freezing' and when he gets back, I'm already somewhere else. I suddenly don't want him in my house. I don't want him to meet Lizzie – 'I hate horses,' he'd said, apropos of nothing. I was quite pleased when I managed to drag him out for a walk around my land and she cornered him next to a blackberry bush and wouldn't let him go. He phoned me from his mobile to say she was bullying him and that he needed rescuing. I wonder if his current girlfriend, the nutcase, even knows he's down here with me, even if it's in a sexless, George and Mildred, John Alderton and Hannah Gordon sort of fashion. When I ask him if I seem different, in any way better, more relaxed maybe, he replies, after giving the matter some thought, 'You seem less mad.'

The night before New Year's Eve we go to a party just outside Simonsbath (it's not pronounced as you would say Simon Dee; it's pronounced as you would say Sim card, without the card bit), at the home of a journalist acquaintance of mine. As soon as we get there, I know he'll hate it: lots of posh people who only 'come down at weekends. That's why we live in Notting Hill, so that we can get to the West Country that much more quickly. You don't live here permanently, do you? Gosh, how on earth does that work? We've got a terrible problem with mice droppings on the pillows ...'

I stand there, looking tall in ripped jeans. He goes quiet. A woman called Pandora, an artist with hair like Kate Bush, says she wants to introduce me to her husband. 'He's standing over there, next to the pistachio Aga.' There are lots of beautiful, willowy teens who I'm sure have never pulled on a pair of jodhs without Lycra, or known what it's like to ride in plimsolls. We leave. I teeter around in the mud in my unsuitable shoes – like my ex-husband, a relic from my old life that no longer fits. He laughs. The drive back across the moor is terrifying: thick fog and ice. Even my sat nav lady has gone to bed, so I keep stopping and peering myopically at signposts. My ex-husband wordlessly reclines his seat as far as it will go and goes to sleep.

I drop him off at the station the next day. He gives me another peck on the cheek; it's like being kissed by a tropical fish, only without the sea. As he shuffles into the station, he is already texting someone else. Well, she is welcome to him, whoever she is. I know I won't be seeing him again. I wonder how you know when you are completely over someone? Is it when your stomach no longer churns when they walk in a room or their name flashes up on your mobile? Is it when you no longer read their horoscope as well as your own? Is it when they send you a text on your birthday, sign it N x, and you think to yourself, who on earth is this? If that's how you tell, then, yes, I'm so completely and utterly over him. Why did I waste seven years on someone who is so impolite he doesn't have it in him to say, 'It's so beautiful here, stunning.' I suddenly feel all defensive about Exmoor, about the smells and the views and my animals. I wish he hadn't come along and spoilt it. For the first time, I almost feel as if it's my home.

I still feel a bit dejected and deflated as I drive back across the moor from the station alone, though. What do I have, really? Even my beautiful modern furniture, my Matthew Hilton sofas and pouffes, my antique armoire from Nicole Farhi, my Eileen Grey glass bedside tables, are lost in the house and don't make up for how awful the interior is. My clothes – my Helmut Lang and Prada suits, my Alberta Ferretti tweed sleeveless dress studded with sequins, my Alaïa jackets and body con cocktails, my Burberry platforms and coat and skirts – are still in their cardboard wardrobes because there is no hanging space:

well, there are awful MDF cupboards full of damp smells, but I'm leaving those unopened for the moment. I used to have all my knickers (by Marc Jacobs, Stella McCartney and Prada) folded neatly, beautifully, in the smooth slidey drawers of my Italian wardrobe and now I don't even know where they are. I thought I was liberating myself from the prison of my perfect life, but all I feel at the moment is in a complete mess. I have a horse I can't even catch in her stable. I have two ponies who have to shiver in a paddock in case they contract a disease I thought only Henry VIII suffered from.

My cats love it here, though, which is the main thing. They are becoming bolder: the other day, I spotted Susie in the hay barn, sat in the rafters, watching the chickens busy-bodying below. Sweetie's always on the muck heap, looking for treasure, her mouth a permanent 'O'. Squeaky, however, only pops out as far as the heather before scooting, glancing over her fat rump in case she is being chased by foxes or swooped on by kestrels, back into the warm. They are like different cats, happy cats, always tired at night from their adventures.

It's now pouring with rain and pitch black and so I slow down as I make my way home. At the side of the road, I spot a shape. It moves. I stop the car and get out. It sits. As I get closer, I illuminate it with the pale blue light of my phone in case it's the beast of Exmoor. It's a sheepdog. Filthy, soaking wet, but definitely a Border collie. He cowers as I put out my hand, but lets me touch him. He is skin and bone. I search for a collar under his great big ruff but I can't find one. I beckon him over to my car.

I think of my cream leather seats. He comes, making a wolf shape. He puts two of his paws on the running board of the passenger side, but can get no further. I scoop him in my arms; he weighs as much as one of my chickens. He sits on the front seat like a person, looking relieved. I strap him in and we drive slowly back home to the farm.

When we finally pull in to the drive, the dog is fast asleep. He is actually snoring. I wonder how long he had been walking along that road and what on earth would have happened if I hadn't found him.

I carry him into the kitchen, placing him on the sofa next to the recently serviced (but definitely not pistachio) Aga. Squeaky, who has somehow made it onto the bread board, hisses but doesn't move a muscle. I don't have any dog food, so I cook some Tilda basmati rice. I go upstairs and run him a warm bath. I place him gently in the water but he's so tired he just lies there, moving one paw as if trying to do breast stroke. I look into his eyes and he understands that I'm going to help him. I shampoo him with Kiehl's Vanilla Shampoo for Normal to Greasy Hair, then pour clean warm water over him. I gather him up in a big black towel – he looks like ET. 'Come on, my darling.' He manages to walk downstairs. I give him a cat bowl of water and the rice, which he swallows in one go. I notice his teeth are tiny stubs, which means the rice grains go everywhere and his tongue keeps popping out of his mouth. I put a pillow on the sofa, then cover it with a White Company sheepskin. He climbs on board. He has very little fur on his back. His black bits are peppered with grey. He has tiny ears, and soulful brown eyes; quite tiny eyes, actually. 'My poor love,' I say. And I switch off the light.

CHAPTER 10

* * *

(In which a goddess in jodhpurs arrives to help me out)

I read somewhere that until the Second World War, because manual labour was so cheap, cavalry horses, which were all confined in stalls, not even loose boxes, were constantly groomed and polished for up to 10 hours a day. The constant fussing and touching literally drove the horses insane. I find it odd that Britain, Australia and America don't take more care of their horses, given the fact that, without their help, not one of these countries would have the riches they have today. The Boer War consumed thousands of horses: the few that didn't die in combat perished through lack of care, lack of feed or disease. The British Government held a royal commission into the problem, and by the First World War a Royal Veterinary Corps was enlisted to care for the horses. The desert campaign used up to half a million equines, while the assault on the Western Front took 1.36 million. Horses were transported by ship to fight abroad – they often suffered dreadfully from seasickness – and if they were not killed in combat, when Armistice Day was declared they were merely left behind. Hundreds of emaciated former British, Australian and American cavalry horses were used as beasts of burden in Egypt. Dorothy Brooke, the redoubtable wife of a British army major-general, arrived in Cairo in 1930 and was shocked to see how these once proud war horses had been forced into hard labour. She formed the Brooke Hospital for Animals, and the charity she founded has gone on to help millions of working equines in developing countries around the world.

I travelled with the Brooke to Ethiopia during my first year on Exmoor and was shocked at what I saw: ponies like skeletons pulling passenger rickshaws for up to nine hours a day in 40-degree heat. There is no limit to the number of passengers they are allowed to pull, no limit to the hours they have to work. I pulled the harness away from one tiny brown pony and could hardly believe what I saw: a seeping wound as deep as my fist, crawling with maggots. I saw tiny donkeys – these are not like Western donkeys; they reach only waist-high, with legs as spindly and hooves as tiny as a lamb's – pulling carts almost improbably overladen with wood, covered in sores from their ill-fitting harnesses, being beaten within an inch of their lives by children. The average lifespan of a donkey in the UK is 30 years plus; in Ethiopia it's just six.

What I will remember most about my trip to Ethiopia is the sight of the grain market, held just outside the small town of Hossana – human population 70,000, equine population 91,040. Mules – half donkey, half horse – are

used for the terrible task of carrying grain because they
are bigger and stronger than donkeys. When I arrived
there were hundreds of mules, heads down, feet spread to
cope with the loads of grain – I worked out each mule
was carrying over 20 stone – while their owners haggled
over prices. There was no shelter from the sun, no water,
no respite. And then, suddenly, the mule standing next to
me went down with a groan. She lay on her side in the
dust, her eyes closed, and I could tell she just wanted to
be allowed to die. She had simply had enough. Her 20-
year-old owner, Abraham, told me they had walked for
six hours in the hot sun to get to the market. I asked him
to take the load off his mule but he refused; he insisted
the mule was just 'resting'. I asked why he couldn't see the
mule was suffering and he told me he believes it's the
mule's duty to serve him. He started to beat the mule to
make her get up, and I turned away. At another market,
I saw a skinny old mare whose tiny, long-legged foal had
been sold and was being pulled away from her by a tight
piece of twine encircling her lower jaw; the foal couldn't
even move her tongue. I watched the mare wandering the
market square, whinnying, calling, desperately looking for
her foal for many hours, until it grew dark, and she fell to
her knees. I thought of my horse back home, how she
hates having a saddle put on too quickly or a girth pulled
too tight. She hates her mane being caught in the brow
band, or the fur on her back being rubbed the wrong way.
How she hates the flies, the hot sun, the cold, the rain,
and how if you show her kindness, she will repay you a
million times over. I thought of Lizzie pulling a cart,

being beaten, being starved, being deprived of even water, and I wanted to do something about these mules and donkeys and ponies, anything. I thought of Dream, and her cross face, her funny ways, her obstinacy, and I imagined her here, in this living hell, being treated as these animals are treated. I wanted to buy the mare that had lost her foal, but was told that there are no sanctuaries in Ethiopia that she could be taken to; even if there were she would have been unlikely to survive the journey.

I had kissed the mule at the market and the men around me had looked at me as if I had lost my mind – here it's rare to see an animal being stroked or even given a kind word. Actually, I didn't see it happen once. What I found most poignant about the plight of these animals is their silence: they don't bray, they don't whinny, they just try their best. When you stand next to them and try to loosen the endless ropes that enslave them, they don't react or bite or move away; it's as if they have completely shut down. Again and again people told me that it's the animal's 'duty' to serve them; that it's God's will. But although the scenes I saw every day were almost Biblical in their antiquity – Ethiopia is the second-oldest Christian country in the world – I couldn't help thinking that God had nothing to do with this. When the nice people working for the Brooke there assured me that, with time, people would begin to understand that the animals feel pain, I snapped at them, 'But Ethiopia is where humanity began. The people here have had time! They have had more than enough time!' I started to wonder whether caring for animals, lavishing all my time and money on horses, is self-indulgent, a luxury. But I only had to look into the eyes of that little brown mare – her name was simply Brown (a black horse here is called, simply, Black) – to know she had a soul, could feel pain, and did not deserve her terrible fate. Her pitiful cries haunt me still.

I was in London on 20 July 1982 when the IRA exploded a car bomb in Hyde Park, killing not only four men, but killing seven horses – Cedric, Epaulette, Falcon, Rochester, Waterford, Yeastvite and Zara – and wounding three others. I had been on my way to the now closed Minema cinema in Knightsbridge, had seen the park closed off, the ambulances arrive for the men. I saw the horses left on the tarmac, the blood on the ground, and I remember the most poignant sight of all was the fact they all still had their saddles and bridles on. To this day, each time The Queen's Life Guard pass the spot where the bomb was detonated, they bring their swords down from the 'slope' to the 'carry' – coupled with an 'eyes left' or 'eyes right' – as a mark of ongoing tribute, respect and remembrance. Horses try so hard for us – I remember those tiny donkeys, picture them when I close my eyes, giving their last shred of strength to the brutal boys who beat them in that hot sun in Ethiopia – and yet we always, always, always let them down.

It's Saturday evening in January and pitch black outside and inside; I don't mean in the house – although I suppose that's true, too, given the stolen light bulb situation –

I mean in my mind. I think all the stars have legged it to another universe. I've named the sheepdog Michael, aka 'Badger'; he has such an impressive white ruff of fur around his neck he also looks oddly Elizabethan. He's sitting in the kitchen, having spent all day softly padding round after me, gently nudging me with his nose if I ignore him for too long. A farmer called Patrick arrived on my doorstep and peered in my hallway (in the countryside, I've found, people just open your front door, willy nilly, even though you might be naked, or busy, or both) and told me he has the 'grass keep' to the land. 'What does that mean?' I asked. 'It means I graze my sheep on your land in exchange for looking after the hedges and the gates, fallen trees, that sort of thing. Plus it helps keep the grass down. You'd be better off keeping those horses in the top field.' I really hate men telling me what to do, and am not overly sure I agree with sheep farming, but I agree to him returning his flock to the fields, figuring I need all the help I can get to look after the place.

I've tried to find out who Michael belongs to. I phoned the local vets and shelters, and scanned websites and newspapers – to no avail. When I took him to my vet to get him checked over (he immediately humped the poor man's leg with a dreamy look on his face – Michael had the dreamy look; the vet appeared mildly alarmed), we found out he's not microchipped, has fleas and worms, and is about eight years old, although we can't be sure of this. The vet told me that with the downturn in farming, lots of sheepdogs are no longer needed and are often just turfed out to fend for themselves. Either that, or Michael just wasn't very good at his job. He is beautifully clean now, but as he is so thin and bald I make him wear a smart navy coat whenever we go outside to keep him warm. He also wears a flashing fluorescent collar: when he motors around the field on our late-night walks to smash the ice on the water butts, he resembles a low-flying, very sniffy UFO. He helps me get Lizzie in and out of the field: he trots at her heels, occasionally taking a mouthful of her tail in his jaws, something she finds very demeaning. I'm feeding him little and often: he quite likes to share my porridge in the morning, the only thing the Aga is good for, apart from defrosting my socks. I realise that although the dog is clean, I haven't washed my hair for a week. I find it too depressing to use the rubber mixer the colour of dentures on the bath, a contraption I hadn't set eyes on since the Seventies. Oh, how I miss my limestone power shower with filtered water, dinner-plate head and side jet washes!

I mix Lizzie's supper, adding a slosh of sunflower oil and cider vinegar and a Nicole Farhi mug of linseed. I've found she loves fruit, although she places the tiny rings of banana carefully to one side. She even likes satsumas, looking all surprised at the first squirt of juice, then smack- ing her whiskery lips with her fat, soft tongue. Having fed the ponies their meagre rations (I feel very mean, giving them so little), I carry Lizzie's bowl into her stable. I place it on the floor and as I walk away I lean towards her neck and plant a gentle kiss below her mane. In a flash, as I turn and make for the door, she swings her head from her bowl and strikes at my leg. The pain is indescribable, probably worse than childbirth, although I suppose at least I'm not lumbered with a baby at the end of it. I sink to the floor, knocked over by the force of her bite and the shock of being attacked. I start to cry and back out of the stable, actually staggering. Probably not the ideal thing to do – you're supposed to get straight back on the horse, etc, etc – but I need to get away from her. I hobble into the house. After all I've done for her! Poor me! I peel down my jodhpurs and examine my thigh. I can see teeth marks from her giant molars, and my leg is already swelling badly. 'You fucking horse!' I yell in her direction, and Michael circles on his White Company sheepskin, looking worried; he hates it if I ever raise my voice, or even bang a spoon on a saucepan.

I imagine this is how parents feel when their privately educated children start injecting heroin. I realise I now own a horse that attacks me when I enter the stable, am always freezing and dirty, my car is filthy, and I will never have sex again! I hate this house, I have no friends, and I'm going to be 50! This is bloody great. The other day, walking Michael down the slope of the big field, I felt a sharp pain in my left knee. Oh god, I thought, I'm going to end up like my mum, although unlike her I don't have any lines around my eyes; I suppose because, unlike her, I've never laughed that much. I was 11 when she first went into hospital, suffering from arthritis. She was having her neck stretched, back then a tactic thought useful for arthritis of the spine. She then contracted it in one hip, then both hips, then both knees. She had numerous joint replacement operations, some more successful than others, and used to joke that she was like the Bionic Woman, but I knew she was always in pain. She is completely immobile now, cared for 24 hours a day by an African nurse who loves her, really loves her, so much more than I do. When I go to see her I can hardly wait to leave, so unbearable, so uncomfortable is it to watch her just sitting in her chair, a forced smile on lips that the nurse has thoughtfully adorned with lipstick. My mum has these stock phrases that she has practised and comes out with in the hope they will fit when she is spoken to: 'I'm getting better.' 'I'm fine, how are you?' And, 'Have you eaten?' I think it was the decade or so of not being able to move much beyond her chair that has made her mind disappear. Maybe it's just as well. At least she doesn't know she's being swung on a hoist from her bed to her chair, butt naked, in front of a window.

I also think I have that disease where you can't experience happiness. How did Henry David Thoreau manage living in a wilderness, alone with his thoughts, apart from using transcendentalist philosophy and making his mum do his washing? Thank you, God, I say, shaking my fist at the sky. I'm reminded of the passage in *I Capture the Castle* where Rose moans, 'I feel grim. I haven't any clothes, I haven't any prospects. I live in a mouldering ruin and I've nothing to look forward to but old age.' And her brother, Thomas, replies rather reasonably, 'Well, that's been the outlook for years. Why has it suddenly got you down?'

But I do feel a bit hard done by. I didn't deserve such an unwarranted attack. I haven't even patted Lizzie since rescuing her from her rutted, freezing field, having read somewhere that horses don't like it; they prefer to be stroked, and scratched on the 'sweet' spot just above their withers. I understand that she doesn't like men, but I had thought she was starting to trust me. I've never done anything to hurt her. Why does she hate me? Why is the Attitude Adjuster not working? I don't go out to see her again that night to top up her water bucket, fill her hay bar and skip out her droppings and set bloody fair. I bolt the front door, fill up my hot-water bottle like an old woman, and climb the stairs, letting out a loud 'Ow!' with every step.

'I hear you need some help with your horse.'

It's two days later. I had phoned Equine Market Watch, a charity based not far from me in Herefordshire that monitors the buying and selling of horses at sales, rescuing those that might be sent to slaughter, and asked their advice. I was told that, perhaps Lizzie being seven and, like Miss Jean Brodie, 'in her prime', and having found her feet in a permanent home, and pumped as she is full of food, was just relishing her role as the 'alpha mare': she was dominating me as she would dominate another horse. 'But I'm not a horse!' I wailed. This was how Nicola the holistic horsewoman had got my phone number.

She sounds lovely, originally from Leyton in east London but having moved down to Somerset to start working with horses a year ago. Basically, she tells me, she looks at horses as a sensitive whole, and tries to think as they do and to treat them as equals. She has owned her own horse since he was three; he is now 12. 'He's never worn shoes, never touched molasses, never had worms,' she says proudly. I wish I was that unspoilt; if only I hadn't plucked my eyebrows, had plastic surgery to reduce my breasts, dyed my hair and mucked up my metabolism with endless dieting I might not be here, now, in a muddy field with an animal that doesn't like me. I'd be doing something more normal, like baking Victoria sponges and putting on a hot wash of children's clothes. 'And Quincy genuinely looks after me,' she adds proudly. 'He is his own person – I don't bully or dominate him – but he would walk through fire for me. I think we knew each other in a past life.'

We arrange for her to come to see me and Lizzie the following day. It turns out she has not been getting a lot of work – she is qualified in Equine Touch, a non-invasive form of horse massage, and Bach Flower Remedies, as well as being an essential oils practitioner – because 'most of the horsey people in Somerset hunt, and I don't agree with hunting'. This is true; even when I occasionally enter my local 'wine bar' – again, how very Seventies – the place is full of stuffed weasels and fox heads and antlers; it's positively macabre. Nic once stopped her car when she saw a hunt in full flight on a road on Exmoor, going full pelt despite the fact the horses were on tarmac and conditions were slippery. Before moving to Exmoor I had thought hunting had been banned, but it seems not. I wonder, not for the first time, how people manage to get away with murder, literally, while if I even dawdle in a yellow box in my car I'm slapped with a fine.

I tell Nic I don't want a relationship with Lizzie where I'm having to constantly tell her off, shout at her, yank her around, keep my distance, give her space and walk quietly on eggshells. I had enough of that living with my husband.

We go into the field. Nic has left her dog, Zac, a Stafforshire cross, in the car. She fondles Michael's triangular ears as she tells me Zac, too, was found at the side of the road, with broken bones and covered in cigarette burns. He's now a little bit of a chavvy dog, with a Burberry collar and jaunty scarf, but so small and sweet and solid, with green slanty eyes, you wonder how anyone would have been capable of being mean to him. I'm reminded of a white pit bull puppy I saw at the cat rescue shelter I got Sweetie from. His young owner had broken his legs and blinded him. 'They were obviously trying to make Zac aggressive for dog fighting,' she says sadly. You can still see where he was burned: he has several small white patches where the hair will never grow back.

Lizzie mooches over and looks in my pockets. 'She is always fine in the field,' I say. 'It's when I tie her up or put her in a stable that she becomes aggressive. She feels trapped.' Nicola, who resembles Lauren, the teenager from the Catherine Tate show, but in a very pretty way, tells me that perhaps Lizzie feels cornered. She's sure she had a bad experience when being trained for racing. 'There must have been a reason she was sold at auction before you found her. Physically, there is nothing wrong with her: she has a short back, great conformation, is well muscled, has blemish-free legs that don't seem to fill or get puffy, and of course she is beautiful. People put up with a lot if a horse is good-looking. It's the ugly ones we have to look out for.'

The problems start when I try to lead Lizzie away from the ponies. First of all, I can't get her headcollar on. I slip it over her nose and she immediately swings away, banging me hard on the top of my head. If I had any neighbours within walking distance, all they would hear me saying over and over again every day is one word: 'Ouch!' When I've eventually got the headcollar on, she won't budge. I pull, she leans back. Even though she has never done Pilates, she's much stronger than I am. When I eventually get her to move, after much clucking and running on the spot to impart that I need energy from her and the strategic use of a carrot, she just circles around me. She pushes me out the way with her shoulders, then swings her quarters at me. 'She has no respect for you at all,' Nic says. 'You're too passive, you're not demanding enough.' Tell me something I don't know. Nic shows me the position I should walk her in: it's safer to be just in front, not at the side where they can trample on you and use their shoulders, although I mustn't keep turning round to check she's still coming, and on no account should I allow her to stop. If she plants, known in horse parlance as 'napping', I must push her off in another direction. To get her to move in the direction I want, I need to twirl the end of the rope. I feel like a multi-tasking cheerleader. Once she has done a couple of steps away from the other ponies, and before she becomes stressed and before I lose the will to live, we take her in an arc back to them. My homework is to do this several times a day, each time increasing the number of steps away from the others.

When we get her onto the yard – the ponies come too, like bodyguards; I should really start getting them to wear dark glasses and use walkie-talkies. 'Lizzie does like to have an entourage,' Nic notices – I demonstrate what happens when I try to pick out her feet. She paws the ground with her front feet, or kicks out with her back ones, like a cow. Then she runs backwards, breaking the baling twine attaching her to the ring on the barn wall; for safety reasons, you never tie a horse's lead rope directly to a metal ring. Lizzie will do anything, in fact, to avoid picking up her feet. Nic feels her all over, and comes to the conclusion, as I had, that Lizzie has a lot of pain in her left, or near, shoulder, probably from overcompensating for the pain in her split feet. She also doesn't know how to balance properly, which is why she's fearful of only standing on three legs.

Nic comes up with a plan to treat the pain: equine touch and flow, followed by a visit from a McTimoney chiropractor called Lindy, and enrolment in a course of clicker training for Lizzie's sticky feet. She takes an orange cone out of her huge bag. There is something a bit witchy about Nic, but in a good way. She recently told me that when she drives home across the moor late at night she can feel the presence of a man sitting on the back seat of her car; he whistles along to the music on the radio but, of course, when she looks round there is no one there. I tell her I have quite enough company with the sat nav lady, thank you very much, but even so, I feel a bit spooked.

Nic believes, as I do, that animals have souls. She used to keep her horse at a livery in Epping Forest, and late one night asked the owner whether she should help her get in the horse that had been left out in the top paddock. 'No, we got them all in. No one's still out.' 'But what about the piebald who's running up and down the fence like a mad thing, asking to come in?' The owner turned a bit pale. Earlier that day, a 22-year-old piebald cob had been too ill to stand and, after much debate, had been put to sleep by the vet. All the horses were indeed in their stables. This reminded me of a story a woman had told me when I was growing up in Essex. She had had to have her old mare put to sleep. The mare had been slowly led out to a corner of the field, where her grave had already been dug; horses are very difficult to manoeuvre once dead. She was stood at the side of the grave and the vet gave her the lethal injection. The horse slumped to her knees and, when she had been pronounced dead, was rolled into her grave, then limestone heaped on top. That evening, the woman returned with her daughter to place some flowers on the spot. The girl whose horse it had been felt a great big shove on her back that made her topple forward. The mare had had a habit of headbutting her in the back, which was annoying but which she would never stop doing. The mare had pushed her from behind as usual, just to say goodbye. Nic recently told me she feels a presence late at night in the barn where we store the hay (the hay barn), as if someone is watching her. I like to think it's just bats, or rats, or Sweetie (although she usually gives a raspy bark to let you know she's there), or insomniac swallows, but I've now started to feel a little nervous when I go in late at night to fetch supplies.

For Lizzie to understand clicker training for her sticky feet she must first learn to be clicker-trained to touch the orange cone. First, Nic nudges Lizzie's nose with the cone, simultaneously giving her a click, followed by a treat. Amazingly, within about five minutes, whenever Nic clicks, Lizzie touches the cone dementedly, wherever it's placed, as though her life depends on it. Every time she touches the cone nicely on hearing a click, she gets a treat. After ten minutes, Lizzie is following Nic into her stable, with no headcollar, no rope, just using the cone. Within a couple of days, Lizzie will lift each foot every time she is touched gently on her shoulder or bottom, and as a reward she will get a click and a treat. Soon the treat bit will be phased out and, eventually, so will the click part. No more wrestling with her (she is, after all, much bigger than me, and will always win); just a gentle touch should bring about the desired response.

Nic then asks about our routine. I tell her Lizzie is brought in at about 6 pm, usually in a J-Lo fashion, i.e. with the ponies. She is then fed, her rugs changed, and left with a full hay bar for the night. At 8 am, she is given breakfast, has her rugs changed again, and is then turned out. The ponies are free to wander off to the paddock, but will generally stay on the yard for a bit, with Benji leaning over the stable door and stealing her hay. Nic wrinkles her tiny nose. Horses were not meant to be confined in boxes, however beautiful and lined with rubber; I've even had rubber stapled onto my stone mounting block. They are meant to move, constantly, interact with other horses in a herd, and play. From now on, unless the weather is filthy, with driving, horizontal rain, she is to be turned out 24/7, just brought in each day for her feed, her homework and a rug change. 'But I bought this place for the stable block!' I wail, and Nic hugs me: it's nice to be touched by another human being again. Usually the only people who touch me are ones I pay handsomely: hairdressers, leg waxers, pedicurists; now that I'm in the back of beyond, the middle of a wilderness, even these encounters are few and far between. 'We'll still use them if the horses need a rest, to lie down or are injured. With all that lovely land, you don't need to keep them in. Horses are not ornaments or cars.'

Next, we go into the feed room. 'Ooh no,' says Nic, leaning into my specially constructed steel feed bins (I've started leaving the odd carrot and banana on a plate on the floor for the rats so they don't feel thwarted), and almost disappearing head first. 'Lizzie is fat, she is not in work, she is in her stable at night, she should not be having conditioning cubes, or Healthy Hooves, which contains molasses.' Feeling like a fatty at a boot camp,

I write down what Lizzie – and the ponies – should be eating: soaked fast fibre, Lucie stalks (which are just chopped grass), fruit, vegetables, their supplements, including Top Spec balancer at £35 a bag, green clay, fresh herbs, and that's it. No oil for Lizzie or the ponies, only half a cup of linseed in winter, and certainly no conditioning cubes. Lizzie is put on a detox regime, which will rid her body of any toxins, allow her to absorb nutrients more efficiently, and also allow her muscles to soften and relax.

Horses, Nic explains, are meant to eat grass, and if we are feeding them anything else we need to stick as closely as possible to their natural diet. I tell her the trouble I'm having keeping the weight off the ponies, and she recommends I soak their hay to remove calories and lunge them every day – or at least walk them down the lane in hand; easier said than done with Dream, who is very much her own person – to shift the rolls of fat. 'I guarantee,' she says, 'we will have Benji off that inhaler and the Ventipulmin within the week. And Dream losing weight will only help the pressure on that pelvis.'

And you know what? She's right. Benji has stopped coughing as though he's about to die and has come off the steroids (he could, theoretically, compete at the Olympics), and Dream is walking not with a spring in her step, exactly, but without pain. Within 10 days of changing Lizzie's diet and turning her out at night, she is like a different horse: she seems calm and, best of all, happy. I still cannot take liberties with her, though: she particularly hates having her rug done up at the front, and will not stand an audience while she's eating, but at least she's not actively trying to kill me. Over the next few weeks, when I get Lizzie in from the field, there's no bucking, no running round in circles and very little napping (or planting), as opposed to sleeping on the spot, although she does sometimes do that too. I still haven't even sat on her, though. Riding, I'm beginning to realise, is turning out to be more expensive and time-consuming than skiing, owning a superyacht or bringing up children.

I tell Nic that I desperately need help with the horses – I still have to work, after all, driving up to London at least once a week to attend fashion shows and the like. I'm wont to imagine I'm Laurence Olivier in *Rebecca*, motoring up to town in an open-top car with a cravat flying, returning late at night along misty roads; the only bit I change is that I don't picture my house going up in flames. Sometimes, my two worlds will clash: the other day, I went to pay in Jaeger on Regent Street, and out of my pocket came a mane comb, a hoof pick and a carrot top instead of my wallet. Nic agrees to bring her horse, Quincy, a Russian trotter, to the yard full-time: he will get free food and livery in exchange for Nic giving me help and sharing her expertise. Once I can get on Lizzie and start riding her, we can hack out together: being with an experienced horse will give Lizzie, and me, much needed confidence.

Nic also tells me that, with work, effort and commitment on my part (oh dear, I feel tired already), there's no reason Lizzie cannot go barefoot. As she tells me more about it, I start to realise how barbaric it is to nail a piece of heavy iron to the base of a horse's hoof. Without a shoe, the foot behaves more naturally as a cushion, absorbing shock and preventing injuries higher up in the leg. A barefoot horse is also less liable to slip, doesn't churn up the pasture as badly, and won't cause as much injury if he or she kicks out. However, I've discovered that even without shoes, when Lizzie stands on my foot (she is always unaware she is doing so, staring into the distance, going 'la la', not noticing me hopping and screaming in pain) my toenails still go black and fall off. I used to have such beautiful feet, I think, looking at them now.

Going barefoot is not a question of just taking the shoes off; nothing to do with horses, I'm starting to learn, is ever straightforward. The hard work comes with the conditioning of the hoof on different surfaces – just walking on grass means the foot is woefully soft – and the daily scrubbing out of the sole and frog (the triangular, spongy part of the foot) to avoid infection. Plus I will have to enlist another expert (all these women seem to have long, grey hair, never wear make-up and swear by the healing powers of Reiki) to trim all the hooves every four weeks, a process that takes much longer than having a shoe replaced. Her feet will be photographed and measured on each visit to ensure progress, that the foot is balanced and growing healthily. The other great plus, of course, is that Lizzie will never again be punched in the stomach by a man. 'Trust me,' Nic says, with a twinkle in her eye, 'you will never go back to shoes again.'

Looking at the sea of mud that surrounds us, the hills,

the cobbles and the flinty paths, and at my own feet swathed in muddy wellies, I'm beginning to realise that neither will I.

CHAPTER 11

* * *

(In which I can put a shovel in the earth, but I sure as hell can't get it out again)

W hen I lived in London, I would eat out two or three times a week: Sunday lunch at the organic pub, and say Friday night at Moro on Exmouth Market, which serves Spanish food – not particularly good for vegetarians, but I liked the ambiance. My favourite restaurant was Rasa in Stoke Newington, a Keralan vegetarian that makes the best black-eyed bean and coconut curry outside the sub-continent. If I had a business lunch, I only had to ring up the Ivy or Le Caprice to be offered my favourite booth. At the Wolseley on Piccadilly, a place where if you turn up saying you'd like something to eat the maître d' looks at you as if you said you've come to do a poo on the floor, I've always found the waiters bow and scrape backwards so ingratiatingly, they remind me of Basil Fawlty when checking in a doctor, a Lord or a Rotarian. Since moving to Exmoor, though, it's as if I've been tipped back permanently into an era before broadband, before computers, even before the advent of Prêts and Starbucks and extra virgin cold-pressed olive oil. None of the pubs are organic and seem to serve only prawn cocktails, things in baskets, rum babas and Black Forest gateau that I can't help thinking has just been thawed and the mouse droppings picked off. Most places, including the chip shop in Dulverton where I sometimes get Snoopy's piece of cod, have 'OAP specials'; something to look forward to, I suppose. No, Exmoor is a culinary wilderness. Not that I've anyone to go out to dinner with, but it would be nice to have somewhere if I did.

In London, I was never one for cooking. I didn't want to mess up my lovely shiny stainless-steel kitchen, for one thing. I never had anything in my cupboards that resembled ingredients – flour, that sort of thing; I can't for the life of me think of any others. If I had the choice between having some toast and circumnavigating the whole affair, thus avoiding the need for crumbs, I'd choose the latter. When I got married, my food repertoire did increase a little. My husband would cook elaborate curries, throwing things around with a nonchalance that wouldn't have seemed out of place were he Keith Floyd, leaving me to do all the clearing up, which put a dampener on the proceedings. Now, though, it looks as if I'm going to have to fend for myself a little bit. I still can't bring myself to eat the chickens' eggs – they produce about one a day; I think they take it in turns – as to do so seems cannibalistic. I tend to break them on top of Michael's food and he laps them gratefully.

I've always liked the idea of eating my own produce: potatoes, tomatoes, peas, runner beans, broccoli. And so, one morning in February, with Michael trotting at my heels, tail a banner, I tramp off in my wellies to the former vegetable garden. I'm hoping against hope that perhaps something has sprouted all on its own to show willing. But no, it's still a square of grass. I recently read a book entitled *The World Without Us*, which examined how long it would take the planet to recover if mankind were exterminated overnight. The book posited several thousand years but, if my vegetable patch is anything to go by, I would say five minutes is more the ticket. There are brambles everywhere. A brick path through the centre has been covered in weeds and grass, and has disintegrated. The gate is off its hinges and the lovely stone walls are buckling under the weight of fern, grass and nettles that have sprung up in every cranny. I pick up my spade, all shiny and new from the garden centre, and smash it into the ground. I get it in okay, and shove it in a bit further by standing on it with both feet. Oh, that I weighed more, I think for the first time in my life. Michael cocks his head to one side as if to say, okay, what next? I wiggle it around and try to pull it out. It won't budge. I pull some more. I heave and I strain. I feel like one of those unsuccessful knights of the round table. I eventually leave it there, hoping no one has seen how pathetic and useless I am, and go back inside the house.

The trouble with all these experts on telly is that they make it look so easy. The reality is so very, very different. I remember what a useless gardener I'd been in London. I couldn't even grow mint. Every year, I would buy colourful, exotic Mediterranean things in pots from the florist, water them spasmodically, they would die, and then I'd buy new ones. And so I ring Brian, the only name and number given to me by the prepubescent estate agent. He lives in Bampton, a picturesque village not too far away, with a wife called Liz who will soon take on mythic proportions. She's a bit like Maris in *Frasier*, always just offstage but with a huge presence: I imagine her in a floral apron.

Brian turns up on a Sunday morning at dawn. He looks very smart in a green military jerkin and plus fours. I think he's been to church. I can't understand a word he says, but I understand from his body language that he used to be the gardener on this property and so knows it inside out. I tell Brian on no account is he to frighten any of my cats (the postman, John, lives in fear of another one of my tellings off about the speed with which he negotiates my lane), put down poison, disturb birds, decapitate any of the animals with his wretched strimmer, or burn anything in a bonfire. I tell him I want the garden to not be too manicured, in order to encourage wildlife. I tell him I want the top paddock to be a wildflower meadow, to encourage bees and butterflies and so that Lizzie and the ponies can go in there to self-medicate on cleavers, borage, nettle, rosehip, wild garlic and chamomile. I tell him I want the trees in the orchard given anti-ageing treatment: propping up trees that are falling down, and planting new ones. I tell him I want the lakes renovated, planted with oxygenating plants, to create a haven for birds, toads and insects. I tell him I don't want him to harm slugs, worms or snails; if they are in the way, they should be rehomed. I tell him that in the vegetable garden I want courgettes, broccoli, broad beans, potatoes obviously, jacket ones and baby ones, red onions, garlic, asparagus (or is that too complicated?), fruit trees, strawberries, flowers for cutting ('I quite like marigolds'), carrots for the horses, salad leaves but no spiky ones, parsley, rhubarb, cabbage, purple sprouting broccoli, sweetcorn, and those green cauliflower things that are all pointy. 'Well,' he says after giving all of the above some thought. I notice he has very few teeth. He wears one of those woollen hats with ear flaps. 'I think I'd better sweep up some of these leaves first.'

The next morning, I wake up to the sound of thundering hooves. I look out my bedroom window to see Patrick the farmer riding a quad bike, two filthy sheepdogs riding pillion, herding his sheep into the big field. Isn't it a shame that all the picturesque things about the countryside – horse-drawn carts, for example – have been replaced. Even bales of straw and hay have now metamorphosed into giant round whorls enshrined in black plastic. There are, literally, hundreds of sheep. Lizzie lifts her head from grazing and immediately sets off in hot pursuit, scattering them, cleaving them like bloody Moses, before trying to stamp on them with her front feet. I pull my jodhpurs over my thermals and head outside, Michael at my heels – he has an expression on his face akin to that on my ex-husband's when he first spotted Emily.

'They're all pregnant,' Patrick says when he spies me. 'Some with twins, some with triplets.' Blimey. Should they be running around like that? Up close, the sheep are very sweet, with very small white teeth and tiny hooves. Some of them lie down, and start re-chewing grass, for the life of them like bored teenagers smacking gum. Patrick asks me to keep an eye on them – like horses, they can get cast, unable to get up – not quite knowing what he is letting himself in for. Over the next few weeks, I would be down in the field, mobile pressed to my ear, describing exactly how 'sheep number 81' was hobbling, 'really quite painfully' or that sheep number 101 was 'really depressed, there's definitely something not quite right'. In the end, with so many of them lame or getting stuck in the stream, I eventually give up even trying to contact him.

A horsebox pulls into the lane, so I go and open the gate. There's never a dull moment here in the countryside. In London, I would go for days without speaking to a soul; here, someone is turning up every five minutes. But, hurrah, it's Nic and Quincy. She gets out, lets down the ramp, and I have my first glimpse of him. He is a very pale grey, with great big dark eyes and huge feet. Very handsome. He shoots off the ramp and Nic leads him down to the Quality Street paddock. We decide to let the horses and ponies get to know each other over the fence – Quincy would probably be fine with the mares, but Benji might get a little proprietorial – rather than throw them all in together. He trots off to introduce himself to the others over the gate. We watch them for a bit, Benji and Quincy squealing at each other like girls, Lizzie and Dream watching, fascinated (if Dream could have crossed her arms and popped her hip I'm sure she would have done so), before going in for a cup of coffee. Five minutes later, Nic says she had better see how they are settling down. We troop down to the gate and, oh my god, Quincy is in the wrong field! He must have jumped the fence to get to the others. As we get nearer, we can see that his legs are pouring with blood. Nic shrieks, and runs as fast as her legs can take her. Quincy is now stood stock still, his head hanging miserably. He must've got caught up in the barbed wire as he jumped the fence to get at Benji: tiny metal shards are still stuck in his leg. We lead him slowly up to the yard. 'My poor horse,' Nic keeps saying. She hoses his wounds, and the vet, Simon, arrives to check him over. He doesn't think there is any lasting damage, unless the tendon sheath has been penetrated. I feel so responsible. Why hadn't I checked for barbed wire? Nic keeps him in that night, nursing him until the small hours. 'It's just horses bein' horses,' she says to make me feel better.

CHAPTER 12

* * *

(In which I mount Lizzie for the first time)

It's now mid-February, and today, a Friday morning, I open my front door to let Michael out (there is no day when I can write: 'There was no possibility of taking a walk that day') and discover that, overnight, we have had nearly three feet of snow.

The sun is shining, the sky is blue, and the effect is dazzling, almost blinding. It's like being in the Alps; the world is muffled, the air clean. I pull on gloves, a hat and thick socks, and we venture out. There are tiny paw prints that could only belong to Sweetie, and a weird, triangular shape made by a big bird. My first job is to get hay to the horses, and to break the ice on their water. There's no way I can push a wheelbarrow through the powdery snow, so I have to carry a bale on my back. Several times, I sink to my knees, wailing to myself that I can go no further. If only the fashionistas on the front row could see me now.

The horses, the gang of four, are all at the gate to the wildflower meadow, whinnying pitifully, looking exactly like a Christmas card. I lever the bale over the gate, and set about dividing it into four neat piles, carefully knotting the twine to dispose of later: if a horse were to eat it, it could easily die. They all play musical piles of hay, Quincy seeing Benji off his, Benji seeing Dream off, Dream putting her ears back and pushing Lizzie, who is twice her size, off her pile. Lizzie wanders forlornly back to the first pile. I always marvel that she is so gentle with other horses, so tolerant, while with humans she is so combative. I think that if I agreed with indiscriminate breeding, and didn't already know there are far too many homeless horses in the world, she would make a wonderful mother. The two horses are dry under their rugs, the Prada of rugs, and their coats have fluffed up so they resemble tumescent teddies. Native ponies, with thick coats, should not wear rugs; the weight flattens their coat, which would otherwise trap warm air, making them colder. Next stop are the chickens, making so much noise in their house it's as though they're holding a conference or coffee morning. I open the hatch and attach their little ramp. Gwen comes out first and promptly disappears beneath the powdery snow. Oh crumbs. I pick her up and place her carefully back inside. Michael cannot walk in the snow as it's so deep, and so he bounces, like a deer. I keep falling over and, having looked at the lane, which is covered in deep, virgin snow, wonder if I'm going to run out of feed for the animals.

Trust poor me to move to Exmoor just in time for its worst winter in 20 years. I start to worry about the badgers in the woods that have had their babies, about the sheep on the hills that don't have the luxury of a shelter, of all the horses left in fields with owners unable to reach them to break their water and give them hay. I immediately set about hanging up fat balls for the birds and refilling the peanut and seed dispensers. The robins, deeply territorial creatures (I now recognise each robin on my land, and know exactly whose patch is whose), have, like soldiers in the First World War on Christmas Day, downed arms so that they can reach the food I've put out for them. On the second morning of being snowed in, I awake to a terrible flapping in my bedroom. The carpet is dusted with feathers, and I see Sweetie in a corner, staring intently at a crouching bird I later identify as a male bullfinch. He looks really fed-up, as if to say, 'I survive the worst snowstorm in 20 years, and then I'm caught by a cat. Typical.' I pick him up and place him gently in an orange Hermès shoebox. I leave him with a bowl of water and some seed, but when I return to look at him a couple of hours later he is dead, his head stuck forlornly beneath the water bowl. When I look bullfinches up on the RSPB website later, I discover their numbers are in decline, and on the red endangered species list. Oh dear.

As I stand on my hill later that afternoon and survey the unblemished view, watching the sun go down, my sheepdog at my side, I realise for the first time since moving here that I'm in what must be the most beautiful place on earth. Lizzie hears us (unlike me, she has ears like a bat) and, leaving her hay and the others, gallops full pelt towards me, mane flying, scattering snow around her.

She's like something out of *Doctor Zhivago*. She only just stops in time, skidding to a dramatic halt just in front of me. I feel her hot breath on my face and I know that she is starting to trust me now, and that I am starting to trust her. For a horse that was so over-bonded she wouldn't move a few steps away from her companions, that she can now gallop towards me with no thought that she's leaving the others behind shows just how far she has come.

Over the next few days, I develop all sorts of terrible, ancient afflictions, including chilblains (oh, the pain!), chapped lips, split hands and athlete's foot. I'd thought all these diseases had, like rickets and polio, been eliminated by new technology. Even though I've had the ancient Aga mended, and each night I light a fire in the sitting room and huddle as near to it as I dare without getting toasted like a marshmallow, the house is so cold. I've been unable to read in bed for long, holding the book with one hand while the other warms up a bit between my thighs, which are now mottled (dappled?) from the hot-water bottle, then swap them over. Do you remember the winter the student spent in Donna Tartt's *The Secret History*? It's like that, except much, much worse. At least he had friends, and youth. Last night I just got in my car, switched the engine on and put the heating up to 30 degrees. Michael, who, whenever I grab my car keys does a little dance with his front paws and insists on getting in and sitting in the passenger seat, got so hot I almost expected him to start sucking on a Strawberry Mivi. The reason I haven't bathed much, apart from wanting to avoid sitting on the dreadful stains in the decrepit bath, is because I can't bear to take my clothes off. If I wash my hair, it freezes. I have felt, all these long, dark months, like Ernest Shackleton walking towards the Antarctic or wherever he was going. If only Michael could behave more like a husky and pull me up some of these hills. I would never eat him, though.

But, after a week of snowstorms, there are some tiny signs that spring is on the way, although the snowdrops that emerged tentatively in January – they peep out in the most unexpected places, like a gift – seem to have gone back down again. There are numerous green shoots peeking out of the now melting snow that I assume are daffodils, tulips and crocuses. Tiny primroses are unfurling their leaves. I heard a cuckoo the other morning. The days are, thank goodness, getting longer. I can now be outside at half past five with no need for a miner's lamp strapped to my head.

Rather optimistically, given the weather and the fact I've never sat on Lizzie, I'm having a saddle made for her. Lavinia, a beautiful woman, again with long, flowing locks, turned up one morning to measure Lizzie's back, which is thankfully wide and unspoilt as opposed to being pinched, and forced into a shark's fin by a too-narrow saddle tree. The saddle will be beautiful, very wide, with suede on the seat, and will cost just over £1,000: that doesn't include the girth, the stirrup irons, the stirrups or the pads that go under the saddle to ensure no pressure is placed on her spine.

Lizzie won't take kindly to something being strapped

around her waist, but then, why would she? I begin to wonder whether, actually, riding a horse is not a form of abuse, a bit like picking up a cat. I hope that Lizzie will enjoy working – hacking across the moor as opposed to eventing at the Olympics or pulling a cart overloaded with bricks in Ethiopia – and that if her brain is kept occupied, she'll be in a better mood, too. I think the same could apply to me.

Nic presents me with a pair of reins she had specially made: they are so light, she doubts Lizzie will even be able to feel them. These we are going to attach to her headcollar, the gentlest method I can think of; putting a bit in her soft, delicate mouth seems barbaric, although I'm slightly worried about being able to stop, especially when we hit open moor.

Lindy the chiropractor had come to treat Lizzie to make sure she was not in pain before having the saddle fitted. Lizzie seemed to understand Lindy was trying to help her. From being a horse who wouldn't even allow me to pick up her feet, to see her with Lindy, her hind leg in the air, being rotated gently, was a revelation, and actually quite moving. Lindy demonstrated a few exercises that I can do with Lizzie each day to keep her supple. First is the mane wobble: I'm to grasp the top of her mane in both hands and gently wobble it. Second is the tail pull. I'm to stand behind Lizzie, grasp the base of her tail in both hands, and gently lean back, keeping my body straight. If ever I see Lizzie standing with one hind leg resting, I'm to hold her hock in my hand, and gently vibrate it. 'Have you ever thought about getting an

Exmoor pony?' Lindy asked me as she packed up all her things. I told her I'd already fallen in love with the ponies on the moor. I love the fact they have a weatherproof coat and a snow chute on their tails. The pony has changed very little since the Stone Age. I had thought the Exmoors were wild, not owned by anyone, but it turns out they have owners, who get them in once a year to check them over, inoculate them, and sometimes send foals and mares to auction. 'I thought they were rare and protected,' I said.

'They are supposed to be protected,' said Lindy, who has her own herd; she lives on a remote farm near Wiveliscombe. 'But, for the first time in over a decade, some mares and foals are going to auction at Bampton Fair this autumn. Can you imagine how frightening it is for a foal to be sold at auction?' I said that, perhaps, the animals will go to good homes, but ponies from the moor have barely been handled, and without a great deal of work and patience, are too wild to make good pets. 'The danger is that they will go for less than £50, which means they are destined to be slaughtered for meat,' she tells me. This despite the fact there are fewer than 200 breeding mares on the moor today.

I'm to start riding using weight aids: I'm first to think about what I want Lizzie to do, then look in the direction I want her to go. This subtle movement will tilt my pelvis, gently shifting my weight in the saddle. So, if I want to circle left, I look to the left, my right hip bone is lowered fractionally, applying the minutest of pressure to her right side. At the same time, my left hip bone is slightly lifted and opened, allowing space for her to move into. You shouldn't be able to see daylight between my knee and the saddle, while my lower legs should just fall around her sides, almost wrapping or hugging her. This method of riding – also called invisible riding or natural horsemanship – is as far away from my riding-school method of kicking, pushing with my seat, pulling the pony in the mouth to stop, shouting Whoa, that sort of thing, as Mr Magoo is from Lewis Hamilton. This is the theory, anyway. At the moment, I'll be happy if I just manage to stay on.

As the moment to actually mount Lizzie looms nearer, I start to get that feeling I had every Saturday morning in the base of my stomach: fear that I was about to be killed. I think there's some link between me trying to quash those fears in my stomach and my teenage anorexia. It was as if, through an iron will and self-denial, I could quieten those gnawing doubts and insecurities. I remember falling off a chestnut pony called Shannon, being winded, unable to catch my breath, thinking I was going to die. I remember falling off a horse called Shadow while I was on a week's residential dressage course in Suffolk, and breaking my wrist.

Why, I think to myself, am I doing this? I had forgotten the fear, remembering only the smells, the creak of the saddle, the romance of riding, until the prospect of sitting on Lizzie became a reality. Why does everyone but me just do things normally? I wish I had more confidence. I wish I could have enjoyed my wedding rather than feeling anxious about the bill and fearful of eating the organic chocolate cake thinking, quite wrongly, as it turned out, that I would soon be having sex; those were the days when I put having food before sex in the same bracket as eating before swimming. I wish I could have relished my role as the editor of a magazine rather than always fearing I would be fired, which I was. I wish I was one of those rosy-cheeked posh girls who always look exactly the same, with or without make-up, who are capable and always get what they want. I remember on that walking holiday in Uttaranchal in northern India, when I had applied my mosquito repellent and SPF 60 sun cream, had my emergency antibiotics stashed in my rucksack, had washed my hands with my antiseptic dry handwash before eating my lunch, was wearing my custom-made walking boots and walking socks, and was accompanied by my guide, my back-up Land Rover, my ground Illy coffee and coffee percolator, not to mention the ever-present anxiety gnawing away in my stomach throughout the entire two-week trip that we would miss the Rishikesh Express back to Delhi in time for our flight, when we came across a blonde public-school type of about 21, who was just standing in flip-flops and shorts halfway up the Himalayas, bossing the locals, telling them how to build a dam, rolling her eyes at me conspiratorially, as if she owned the place. Why can't I be more like that, I wondered enviously? Can it be learned, acquired, or did I have to have gone to public school and have a mummy in a twinset?

First, I have to get on Lizzie. I have to do this or I might as well just move back to London. I strap on my back protector and pull on my crash cap. Lizzie, having shimmied throughout, is now tacked up. The secret to tacking her up is to do the opposite of what instinct tells you. As I place the girth around her tummy, she moves away; but rather than letting the girth drop until she stands and then trying again (which teaches her that every time she stands still something horrid will happen), I keep the girth on her side as she moves. When she stands stock still, I take the girth away from her side as a reward; not much of a reward, granted, but it seems to work. I do the girth up slowly, in increments rather than pulling it tight all at once. When she finally has all her bits and bobs on, which takes about an hour, she looks very smart – just like a racehorse, in fact, although, unlike a racehorse, which has a short, even mane, hers is long and flowing. Horses' manes and tails are never cut, don't ask me why, but are instead 'pulled' – the long hairs are plucked from underneath, rather like an enormous and laborious leg wax, which all sounds rather painful to me. There are so many rules when it comes to riding horses, such as that you should mount from the left or near side, never the right. This came about because officers in the cavalry always carried their swords on their right side. But I've had enough of rules. Horses need their manes and forelocks for protection from flies, the sun, hedges. Tails shouldn't be narrow and pulled at the base, either, as a great big, bushy tail protects their delicate bottoms from bites from other horses and those dreaded summer flies.

The first job is for Lizzie to stand next to the mounting

block, which is easier said than done. She either stops too far away, so that I would have to swing like Cheetah to get in the saddle, too far forward or too far back. Every time she gets it not quite right, Nic walks her in a great big circle so that she can try again. I think of the sight of racehorses being hauled, straps around their backsides, hoods over their heads, into the starting pens before a race, their bodies quaking with fear. Very often, a panicked horse can rear in the starting pen, and injure itself, sometimes even toppling over backwards. I wonder why no one bothers to take the time to teach them to do it calmly, without any fear.

At last, after two or three tries, Lizzie has stopped in the right spot. The moment of truth has arrived. I swing my leg over her deliciously round rump, and land gently in the saddle. She looks worried; her ears are back. Nic stuffs her front end with apples. I sit quietly, reassuring her by rubbing her sweet spot. I had forgotten how different the world looks through a pair of ears. She is wondering what on earth I'm doing back there. Generally, if something is on a horse's back, it's about to eat them: horses are prey animals and by nature would at this point take off. Lizzie has decided to trust that I know what I'm doing. I ask her to walk a few steps forward. First, I think forward. I don't push her with my seat, nor do I close my legs. I open my hands on the reins (I'm always supposed to be able to see my nails), although I've taken up very little contact anyway, as Nic is at her head, and racehorses have been trained to do the opposite of normal horses: if you tighten the reins, holding them together, they simply think they have to go faster.

Lizzie is worried about carrying me: not only is she not used to my weight on her back (although I'm not, as my ex-husband would have had you believe, 11 stone, I'm more like nine), she's worried she isn't wearing shoes. When ridden, barefoot horses wear special, and hugely expensive, boots, and we have placed these on her feet: they have pads in the sole and inflatable cushions that hug her heels; pumping her boots up made her feel quite like a bicycle. Even so, she believes that if she moves her feet will hurt. I let her think about it for a couple of minutes. This is something else I have learned from Nic: all too often, you see riders hurrying their horses, not giving them the chance to look around them, take it all in. This is why a horse shies at an unfamiliar object: the rider has yanked its head and made it rush past something, whereas if you allow the horse to stop, turn its head and have a good sniff, nine times out of ten it will just decide something isn't scary at all and will walk calmly by.

Having been given the time to work out what's happening for herself, Lizzie decides to take a small, tentative step forward. I give her huge encouragement. She takes another one. Then another one. Great praise, and as a reward I get off her, slowly and gently. My knees are weak. Lizzie looks all proud. Marvellous. I think of the horses who were 'broken' by being tied to a heavy lorry tyre until they either stopped fighting, or broke their neck or a leg. I think of Black Beauty and poor old Ginger.

We did it. We did it gently. I undo her girth and slide

the saddle off her back; underneath, she is sopping wet, telling me how stressful she found the whole ordeal, and how in spite of this she was able to control herself, and stand stock still. What a good, good horse.

CHAPTER 13

* * *

(In which Michael eviscerates a sheep)

It's odd, but I keep finding sheep with nibbled ears or bruised lips. Once, I found a very small sheep stuck in the mud of the stream in the wood. Michael had alerted me to her predicament. Having lost him during our morning walk, I followed his barking, and finally found him stood next to her, looking very waggy indeed. He was also up to his tummy in mud. 'Good boy!' I told him. He wriggled contentedly. I decided there was nothing else for it but to get in the stream and lift her out. I put my arms around her thick, bouncy middle. I pulled. I fell over. I was covered in mud. My Dolce & Gabbana sweater is not what it was. I tried again, and this time I got a good grip. The sheep bleated, and looked surprised and embarrassed. I noticed her ears and muzzle were bleeding. 'Oh my goodness,' I said to her. 'Have you been caught in the barbed wire? Has a fox been after you?' I'd noticed a big male fox walking across my lawn a few days before, and had started to worry that Squeaky might just get stuck in the cat flap at an inopportune moment. I pulled her out (the sheep, not Squeaky, who instead marched indignantly around the house wearing the cat flap as a skirt for a little while), and we both landed on the bank, exhausted, wet and covered in leaf mould. We looked as though we'd been shipwrecked.

The sheep was so dirty and exhausted I decided I couldn't leave her there and so I lifted her, and started to stagger up the hill with her in my arms. I had to keep stopping to put her down and rest. She was very good, just sitting on the grass like a pile of washing until I was ready to pick her up again. Michael was trotting along, leading the way, trying to help. I got to the stables and placed her in Lizzie's now empty box, gently setting her down on the straw. I got her a shallow bowl of water, in case she wanted to drink lying down, and a section of hay. I phoned the farmer. About 10 minutes later, he arrived on his quad bike, sheepdogs riding shotgun. He went into the stable, picked her up by a back leg, and plopped her in the small trailer. He gave her an injection for the wounds. And that was it. I'd have thought she would at least have been handwashed and dried flat.

It's early evening and I take Michael for his walk. I love our evening walks: all the hard, back-breaking work is out the way – the soaking of hay, the shovelling and wheeling of muck and, now the horses and ponies are barefoot, the scrubbing of all the feet with Hibiscrub. It costs £35 a container, and I currently use more than the NHS; I'm beginning to feel as though I own a millipede. (I think the only time my ex-husband ever made me laugh was when I told him he didn't have a leg to stand on over something or other and he grinned and said, 'Yes I do. I'm a millipede.') The feet must then be allowed to dry thoroughly before Field Paste, an antiseptic water barrier at £15 a tiny pot, is massaged into their crevasses. Honestly, Mariah Carey has nothing on these animals, whereas I barely have time to drag a curry comb through my hair and brush my teeth.

We cross the stream and follow it beside the hill field. Michael disappears as usual, but I'm not remotely worried: he's probably chasing a pheasant. I continue walking. I get to the gate to the lane – no sign of his black and white tail. I call him. Nothing. I retrace my steps, annoyed and hungry, and about half an hour later, I hear him barking. I tramp towards the sound. I spot him. He's in the stream, next to the lake. I go down to him, slithering inelegantly, hanging onto the roots of trees. 'What on earth are you doing?' I ask him. I always address animals as if they were people. 'Come on, I've got a baked potato in the Aga.' He is again stood next to a sheep. Again, the sheep is tummy-deep in water, bleating plaintively. 'Oh bloody Norah,' I say. 'This is getting ridiculous.' I try to call the farmer, hoping he can just come and sort it out, but his mobile goes straight to answerphone.

I wade into the stream, and again I put my arms around the sheep's waist. I give it a tug, and it moves a little bit and lets out another bleat. I realise how often I've sounded exactly like that. 'Come on,' I say to her. I give her another tug, and with huge effort lift her out of the water, up onto the bank. As I let go of her, I see that my left hand is covered in blood. I peer over at her other side. The whole of her left flank has been torn open, right through the wool. I can see her intestines. She must be in such tremendous pain. She tries to walk, but cannot. I take off my sweater, still the same one, still £500 worth of Italian design, place it on the mud, and lay her on it. Michael is by now beside himself. I ask him to sit (I don't agree with telling animals what to do; I hate it when you see a dog being walked in London, trying to sniff, as dogs do, and the owners keep yanking them by the neck, saying, 'Come on!'). He tries to nudge me, and as he does so I notice that his muzzle and his teeth are covered in blood. 'Oh no,' I say to him. 'Oh Michael.' He gazes at me with sorrow, shame, joy, a bit more shame, and love.

I know, now, that it was Michael who chased this sheep into the stream, and then bit and bit and bit at its tummy until she couldn't stand it any more, Michael has so few teeth, I'm surprised he hadn't just sucked the poor thing to death. I climb to the top of the bank to use my phone again. I know now that Michael tried to do the same to the first sheep. I'm too scared to phone the farmer and am already thinking of how I can hide Michael, as if I'm from the French Resistance and he is an escaping Allied soldier. And so I call the vet. It goes to an emergency answering service. I explain where I am, and how to get there. I go back down to sit with the sheep. I stroke her head, covered in its cream afro. She closes her eyes and bleats softly. After what seems an age, but is in fact only 10 minutes, a 4x4 appears in the field. The vet, a lovely young Polish woman, gets out and runs to us, clutching her bag. She is quite rough with the sheep, and pokes her wound. 'Can you save her?' I ask. 'I don't think so. She's in shock, and there are puncture wounds that have penetrated the intestine, so the infection will already have taken hold. I think it's best that we put her to sleep.'

I sit, the sheep's head resting in my lap, Michael banished to high dudgeon (a grassy knoll), and the vet gives the sheep a lethal injection. The sheep closes her eyes. After a few moments, she stops breathing. The vet listens to her heart, and says that she is gone. I don't think I've ever felt such a wash of sadness come over me in my life, not even when my dad died, which is odd, and shameful. While I'm sitting in the mud with the dead sheep, I think of when I sat in the back seat of the black limousine with my mum, probably the only time she has ever been in a limousine, the hearse in front of us, and my mum saying, 'I can't believe my poor, poor darling is in that coffin.' My face is now slicked with tears; the vet obviously thinks I'm insane. She stands up slowly, shakes an aerosol can and sprays the sheep with purple dye, alerting the farmer to what has happened so that the body doesn't end up in the food chain. At least, I suppose, the sheep wasn't driven hundreds of miles to be slaughtered in an abattoir, but I'm so cross with Michael I can barely look at him. He's doing his Gromit stance. Now I know why he was abandoned, starving, next to a road in the middle of an Exmoor winter.

I call the farmer the next morning to tell him what happened, offering to pay for the sheep, and telling him where we left her body. He says that, if Michael is found loose among sheep again, he will probably be shot. 'You can't cure a dog like that when he's gone bad,' he tells me. 'They get a taste for it. He'd be better off living in a flat in London, where there are no sheep within miles.' Oh bleeding hell. I wondered how long it would take before the locals started shunning me and telling me to get my city arse back to the Big Smoke. I think of Alan Bates in a smock, and the scene where the sheepdog inexplicably herds his charges over the cliff to their death. A few months later, the sheep's body is still there, the wool daubed with purple. No one has bothered to move her. In the end, all that is left are a few glistening white bones.

CHAPTER 14

* * *

(In which I no longer wish to live in Waynetta Slob's clothes, or her house)

It's now early March, and the garden and fields are a riot of blossom. Even the tired old apple trees are covered in pink and white flowers – what once were twigs are now displays so extravagant they wouldn't look out of place in the lobby of Claridge's. A wisteria, which had been there all along but I just hadn't noticed it, is dangling heavy, heady purple flowers outside my bedroom window. The peach and pear blossom is spectacular, but the quince tree outdoes all the rest: its tiny flowers are a deep, hot, Valentino red. When I stick my head out my bedroom window late at night and breathe deeply it's like being at a wedding, or a funeral of someone who will be much missed. There are daffodils everywhere: in the woods, on the lawn. The cats keep coming in from the garden with their heads dusted with yellow pollen, like mini Picassos. There are so many honey bees buzzing around the front door, where there is a spiky shrub with tiny red petals, I feel I'm in a Bradford Dillman movie. The bumble bees seem drunk; I almost expect them, as they hover past as if in slow motion, to start singing pub songs. The hedgerows, which are about four feet thick and as tall as a man, are bursting with life: there are unfurling ferns, foxgloves, wild garlic, extravagant cow parsley as lacy as a wedding veil. I've even seen my first swallow: she has been in the tack room, cleaning out the debris in an old nest, a bit like Sarah Beeny trying to renovate her way up the property ladder. The hens love the longer days: they bask in the sun, spreading their wings, bliss written all over their tiny beaks.

There are so many things about relocating, relocating, relocating to the countryside that no one bothered to tell me about – not Phil, not Kirstie, not bloody Kevin McCloud. I find out from Patrick the sheepfarmer that I'm entitled, as a landowner, to an annual payment for the upkeep and conservation of the land. When I phone my conveyancing solicitor to ask her about this, and to say that I was supposed to have had something called, you guessed it, the 'entitlements' to the land handed over to me upon completion, she denies all knowledge of such a thing. 'The vendor didn't disclose that to me,' she says, over and over again, like a robot; maybe she is a robot. No one told me that, before I lag the loft or repair the roof to the hay barn and stables – water pours in all the time, soaking the rugs and the bedding – I need to employ a team of accredited ecologists to find out whether there are any resident bats in the rafters, what species they are, their inside leg measurements, and to map their flight paths. Only then, I'm told by an officious creature at Natural England, will I be able to purchase a licence to disturb them. I will then have to build a special insulated loft just for them to move into above the stables, which will have a trapdoor entrance with a sign saying, 'Do not enter: roosting protected long-eared bats' and a clause written into the deeds of the property protecting them in perpetuity. The cost of this special insulated loft dwelling for the bats, never mind the cost of the fleets of experts who will monitor the proceedings, is £26,000. The woman at Natural England warns me that if I don't do all of the above. I will be 'committing an offence'. Can I at least get the septic tank emptied? 'Not if you might have newts,' she wittered hysterically.

I find this whole stance odd, duplicitous and contradictory. Why are we all allowed (well, not me, obviously, but most people) to eat pigs and lambs, to shoot male calves in the head the day after they are born (they are not valuable if born to dairy cattle), to keep horses in conditions where they are starving, treading on the bodies of other dead horses; the case of Spindles Farm springs to mind: 32 horses were found dead, over 100 were found severely emaciated, unable to walk at a farm in Buckinghamshire. The owner had paid as little as £1 for equines destined to be slaughtered, their meat sold abroad. Why are we allowed to shoot deer, rabbits, rooks and foxes with impunity, to experiment on primates, to keep chickens in a space the size of an A4 piece of paper, but bats, which I wouldn't have dreamed of harming anyway, need an insulated loft built for them? The roof they are living in already, where they hang upside down, moving their little capes as they shift in their sleep (they really are awfully sweet; mine are pipistrelles and horeshoe bats), is falling down, missing numerous slates, and battered with wind and rain. If I'm not granted a licence to repair the stables and the barn, the buildings will fall down, and the bats will move out anyway. What, I wonder, would the bats have done before humans were invented?

However, I've been making some limited progress on the ghastly Stella Gibbons-worthy house. I've had enough of waking every day in a deep, dark gloom, dressing like Kathy Burke as Waynetta Slob and shuffling around in her house, Steptoe-like mittens on my poor chapped hands. All those fashion designers and the nice people at M&S lied about cashmere: it's not warm at all. I realise I have to keep my standards up a bit, even though the only people I ever see are Nic, her Buddhist younger boyfriend, Kevin, who comes down from his investment banking job in London to sweep the yard at weekends, Emily and Brian (Brain; even he has decided to try dentures).

Now the weather is a half a degree or so warmer, I've got the basics done: I've had an oil tank installed (£4,000 to fill it); Black Mountain sheep wool lagging laid (after a great deal of negotiation with the wretched bat people, the building regs people and the local organisation set up to help homeowners eliminate their carbon footprint) in the enormous loft (very ecologically friendly, but £4,000; I could have bought a complete new spring/summer outfit from Marni for that, and still had change for some shoes. Or, hell, just lined the loft with Marni sweaters and have done with it); and a central-heating boiler fitted with a great big water tank, which means I should, hotel like, never run out of hot water (an unimaginable, infinite number of pounds spent in order to ensure that).

I've had all the manky radiators replaced with reclaimed steel school column ones, and all the wiring redone, which means I now have smart steel sockets and switches rather than dirty old plastic ones; the plumber is proper crumpet, as Nic would say, but also has a wife and children who live in the village. Using my fingers, I calculate that he is also young enough to be my son, if only I hadn't been knee-deep in ponies and had discovered boys at a much younger age. The point is, he's out of bounds, but he's a reminder that I'm a sexual being, or could be had I not decided to hibernate like a hedgehog; I've been told I'm also as prickly as a hedgehog, so a fairly good analogy all round. And I've started to rip up the carpet, finding beneath it by turns flagstones (on the ground floor and in the cellar, where I also found a safe I can't open, and one bottle of screw-top wine) and wide oak boards (upstairs – why on earth would people cover them up, especially in the bathroom?). I've yet to have the rooms decorated, but plan on dark, beeswaxed floors, pale grey walls and modern lighting. Because the cats have become so fond of the carpet and cling onto it desperately as I roll it up and give it to Brian to put on the bonfire (which he has to poke many times with a stick before he lights it, in case some poor creature has taken a shine to it), I'm going to have to put down a few rugs, too.

My bedroom is already looking better: I have three column radiators, one under each window (did I mention the room is dual aspect? It means it gets lashed by wind and rain twice as often), my plasma TV is on the wall above the fireplace (not that I ever have time to watch it; come 9 pm I fall asleep, fully clothed and starving), and I now have a cascade of huge light bulbs forming a chandelier in the centre. The awful peeling Seventies wallpaper has been steamed off by the lovely builder, and the walls replastered. I'm now waiting for the plaster to dry. Once I've hung chocolate brown velvet, cream-lined curtains and polished the wooden floor, I will, I'm sure, feel so much more at home and tranquil, more like me and much less like Waynetta Slob.

Off the hall, which has now revealed its worn flagstones (who, I ask you again, would put beige fitted carpet over mellow brown stone?), I plan to have two sitting rooms: to the left a more formal room with two matching raspberry velvet chesterfields and a log-burning stove, and French windows opening onto the patio. A cosy room will be to the right, with a huge fireplace you can sit in and my distressed leather Nicole Farhi club chairs (I have two; I was hoping they might breed). My office is next to the kitchen – it will have the shutters replaced, be lined with books and have its flagstones exfoliated – and beyond that I'll have a dining room in what is now, laughably, called the 'cold room', as if this house contained anything but: it used to be the dairy, and still has just wire on the windows instead of glass, and hooks hanging from the ceiling from which game was once hung – I'm going to get rid of these.

The separate wing of the house, called the Cider House, is just two horrid, damp rooms. Somerset Council, in their wisdom, and despite the fact they've been along to inspect it and have seen that it's just two tiny damp rooms, charge me a completely separate council tax for it. I'm one small person, whose leftover sprout peelings and carrot tops are eaten by a multitude of different beasts of the field, but still I pay as much in council tax as two huge extended families with no pets at all and a junk food habit that means they will, ultimately, all of them, prove a drain on NHS resources. I'll knock through the two rooms, creating a downstairs utility room where I can wash horse rugs, Lycra horse aerobics gear, dog towels, dog coats, muddy jodhpurs and so on and take off my wellies. I'll also have a larder: I still don't have any ingredients, I just like the old-fashioned, Nigella Lawson idea of it. A new staircase from that room will lead upstairs to a tiny snug.

The bathrooms – there are two upstairs and just a cloakroom downstairs – are going to be renovated and fitted with antique, free-standing showers, iron tubs and reclaimed sinks. I've gone off that modern, egg-shaped bath, Philippe Starck taps and pale limestone look that can routinely be found in hotel bathrooms around the globe; they become dishevelled and splashed in an instant. And while I had thought I'd spend £30,000 I don't have on a Bulthaup kitchen – I still hanker after another Sub-Zero fridge – I now think I'll just hire a van, drive to Wales and buy an old dresser and a huge, worn oak table with drawers with cupped brass handles. I've decided never again to have a house that isn't comfy, that only looks good when everything is hidden away, that you are a slave to and worry about in case someone comes to visit and drapes a cardi on a chair. I want the house to be resilient, to be a bit shabby and worn around the edges. A bit, I suppose, like me. I've decided to keep the horrid cream Aga – I've grown used to its gentle, reassuring warmth, like a mummy. I know it's very non-environmentally friendly, but I figure I've never had children and so deserve a few carbon credits to make up for that bleak fact.

The big news is that, in the second orchard, the slightly more menopausal Thora Hird one, I've had an outdoor school built for the horses. I was supposed to obtain permission to remove the two old, dead apple trees but I just got Brian to cut them down and I burnt them in the sitting room: the smell of apple logs is delicious, like sitting in front of a huge, warm crumble. The surface of the manège (not ménage; there is, unfortunately, no sex going on here at all) is sand (I had to ferry a tiny crab, who was tipped out with the load, back to the beach at Minehead to release him; he didn't even look that grateful as he sidled off), topped with reclaimed shredded rubber, perfect for conditioning Lizzie's hooves, and very safe to ride on. I can now take Lizzie down to the school, mount her from a stool (if you get on from the ground you are placing too much strain on a horse's back; cowboys, be damned), and walk her round in different directions. After several weeks of this, all the while with me saying, 'Calm, calm,' I've also started to tentatively trot her. At first, she didn't want to unseat me too much, sensing I was none too secure, and so she just moved her feet while keeping her body perfectly still. Now, though, she does a lovely trot, with a relaxed head and perfect curves on every corner: I'm supposed to just be able to see the lashes of her inside eye. If she rushes, Nic, who is stood in the middle of the school, for all the world like a ringmaster at a circus as I whirr round her, tells me to do a half halt. This is a squeeze on the outside rein, not a pull back on both reins, which will only make her stop or excite her, causing her to gallop off into the distance. Lizzie is incredibly sensitive and responsive. If I think 'trot', she trots. If I think 'slow down', she slows down. It's as if, like Derren Brown, she can mind-read but I guess she's just reading the subtle signals from my body. If I want to turn left, I remember to look to the left so my head turns, my shoulders follow slightly and the weight in my pelvic bones shifts so she knows to move, too. I try very hard not to unbalance her, to keep my hands quite high and soft because she is so green and I don't want to give her a bad experience. I try not to visualise her taking off, careering round and round the school like a motorbike.

I've also worked her in the manège from the ground, free-schooling her (without attaching her to a lunge rein, which could pull on her delicate head), so that she learns to listen to my voice commands. She loves this: she trots as though she is floating, and if I ask her to canter she puts in an enormous flying buck, all four feet off the ground, adding a corkscrew twist just for good measure.

So that she doesn't become bored, I've also been taking her for walks down the network of hedge-flanked lanes; it's like leading a giant dog through a maze. So far we've met tractors, combine harvesters, cars and people out with dogs, and she has taken them all in good humour. Walking with a horse is a great bonding exercise: I chat to her, she listens and she learns to trust me. Whenever we get to a puddle, which is about every three seconds, she puts her nose close to it and blows, creating ripples that frighten her so much she jumps back a half a step. She is so beautiful, she makes my heart expand. She's also very nosy, peering sideways into the windows of cottages as we go by. I sometimes catch glimpses of families eating lunch, leaning across each other rowdily at a table, and feel desperately odd (I meant to type odd there, but I could just have easily have typed old) and alone. I miss my normal life, when I would get up late at weekends, wander around in my pyjamas and a T-shirt without fear of frostbite, watch an afternoon film, order a takeaway, have a drink with a friend in the trendy bar of a hotel and not feel out of place. I wonder what people would think if they looked in at me now, sitting on my sofa next to the fire, in a mad outfit of layers (jodhs, waistcoat, leggings, socks, leg warmers, scarf, dressing gown, parka), Squeaky in a puddle on my lap, Michael sat upright beside me. I'm sure I'm known variously in the village as the 'mad animal lady' and the 'townie from hell'. Ah well.

CHAPTER 15

* * *

(In which I wish there was a tiny bit of romance in my life)

I decide to take Michael to the beach for the day. I put him and a towel and a couple of his toys on the back seat of my car, but straight away he comes forward to the front, giving my left ear a wash in the process. We drive across the moor until we come to a sign for somewhere called Woody Bay; the road is just one track, with a sheer drop on one side. I manage to park and we walk down the long path to the beach, for all the world as if in a Daphne du Maurier novel; there is even a little house in the cove. But there is a sign saying 'No dogs after March'; damn – we're now in April. Despite the fact there's not a soul about, I decide that if we're not wanted, we'll go elsewhere.

We get back in the car and head west. I see a sign to Saunton Sands, which rings a bell. We drive through Barnstaple (not the prettiest of places, with too many roundabouts – do they really think the tulips in the middle make these scars on the landscape less ghastly – and car parks; why did the British have to ruin all the market towns?), and take a tiny road to the beach. We park outside rows of shops selling spades, rubber rings and tiny red buckets (do children really still want all this stuff? I'd be really heartened if they do), and look up at the cliffs. There, on the very top, is the Saunton Sands Hotel, a monument to 1930s architecture and a far gentler age, when all holidaymakers wanted was some sea air and a good blow; not a spa, not hot weather, not nightclubs, not even a pool, just the salty sea air. I now know why the name rang a bell. In my mum's bedside cabinet, she has a postcard from my dad, sent in the summer of 1940. He had sent it to his mum in Mill Hill, north London, saying he was 'very fit, and enjoying great weather'. He had been home on leave and had gone to court my mum at Saunton Sands; her father was a doorman at the hotel. As I walk Michael, I imagine the two of them sauntering hand in hand, her in a floral dress from Horrocks, him in his army fatigues and beret and Sam Browne belt, both in their early twenties, both in love, optimistic, planning a future despite the fact there was, as my mum was always saying, 'a war on'.

Although the clean air is in my face, and 'my new boyfriend' is frolicking in the pools of water left behind by the tide (from his reaction – leaping in the air whenever a wave comes towards him, trying to prise clams from their moorings in rockpools – I don't think he's ever been to the seaside before), I feel deflated. Why doesn't someone love me like my dad loved my mum? I know I didn't find my perfect, empty, cheated-upon life in London fulfilling, but do I find this one any better? Do I? I just don't know. So much isn't how I imagined – it's all so much harder (I'm bleating again, like a sheep). I miss my dad at this moment: he was always there to give me advice, to tell me when my car needed a service, and which was the best route to take whenever I went on a journey. He and my mum lived in a more civilised, romantic age. As a young married couple they thought nothing of driving from one end of the country to the other in a blizzard in a broken-down Morris Minor just to attend a cocktail party. They weren't always worried, although they had plenty to worry about. They weren't overly concerned with having *things*. My mum had a good dress, a good pair of shoes and a pair of jet earrings she snapped on her lobes with a gesture that reminds me of Liz Taylor; pierced ears are nowhere near as sexy. She didn't have a million handbags, she had one. But still she was loved.

Why, I wonder, when I have so much, and have, on the outside, achieved so much, am I so scared all the time? Of everything? First it was ponies, then it was school, boys, discos, growing up, college, exams, work, travelling for work, being fired and not having any work, getting married, being abandoned, being cheated on, losing my house in the divorce, growing old. And now it's people who might spot my dog on a beach and, finally (I could insert a lot more topics in this list, but I don't want to take up too much space), I'm back to ponies yet again. I've come full circle. I've realised – a bit too late, I suppose – that you cannot find peace just by moving to somewhere peaceful.

I'm in love with Lizzie, of course I am. I go to bed thinking about her and I wake up longing to see her. The first thing I do when my alarm goes off is to extricate myself from beneath the still sleeping commas of Susie and Squeaky and look out my bedroom window to see if I can spot her. If she's in the wildflower meadow (oh, how miserably this little square of scrub is turning out. Nature, left to its own resources, even with the helping hand of several hundred tiny, hand-reared, organic rare plugs of native breeds inserted lovingly with a dibber, can be very stubborn and ugly sometimes. The only colourful thing that has sprouted in this field so far is yellow ragwort, which can be fatal to horses and has to be pulled up by its roots and burnt), she will raise her head mid-chew and whinny at me. If, as a child, I'd seen her on our suburban lawn, how overjoyed would I have been, how complete. I wonder if we should be more careful what we wish for. I wouldn't give Lizzie or any of the animals up now, of course, but I wish it wasn't all such hard work, so expensive, so slow, so disappointing. I'm not just talking about the wildflower meadow, but about the fact it has taken so long for Lizzie to behave in any way like a 'normal' horse, about the fact Benji was so ill, Dream is so disabled, and Michael so dangerous to leave around sheep. I'd wanted a dog I could just allow to roam in and out the house as he pleased, who would snooze on the lawn, not one who had to wear a lead and a muzzle. It's all so ridiculous and not how I thought it would be. Why does everyone else seem to sail through life whereas I flail about in a leaky row boat without a paddle?

But, on the other hand, I know I cannot go back. I cannot just sell up (God, with the economic downturn, having bought at the top of the curve, I would end up with nothing, less than nothing, if I sold the farm now) and move back to London. I couldn't give up my animals, and anyway the cats wouldn't look kindly on being relocated yet again. They have come to love the hollow trees they can hide in, pouncing on me unsuspecting as I hang out the washing (I'm the proud owner of a washing line, you will be pleased to hear; the scent of my fresh, country air-dried sheets reminds me of holidays, picnics, and taking my A levels). Watching Michael playing on the sand, digging up stones, racing back to me garlanded with seaweed like a hula-hula girl I dread to think what would've happened to him if I hadn't moved here. I dread to think what would've happened to any of the other animals, come to think of it.

I shouldn't be expecting anything back at all. But there are times when I want to share what is happening in my life. Not just the bad bits, the muddy bits, the expensive bits, but the wonderful bits, too. This view, here now on Saunton Sands, seems wasted on just poor me, on my own. I have been trying to work out the last time I had sex. It must have been the summer of 2007, on the couple of occasions I got together with my ex-husband while he was trying to 'win' me back. And, right now, I am starting to think I will never, ever do it again. Now, I know I'm going against decades of dreaming about the prospect, wanting it, going to extreme lengths to get it (I once moved house just so that I could live next door to someone I fancied. I threw a party so that I could invite him, decorated the garden, exfoliated myself until my skin was raw, and then he got off with my friend Wilma, who had turned up in an old frock and plimsolls and hadn't even washed her hair), but once I started to have sex, I found the whole business quite tiring and repetitive, to be honest. It's such an odd thing to do. And now, well, I'm so hopelessly out of practice, and believe myself so unattractive and past it that I'm as scared by the prospect (no, there is no prospect other than a theoretical one, please don't get excited) as I was aged 19 when I went on that skiing holiday in Montgenèvre with my friend Sue Needleman and a really gorgeous French boy named Michel tried to have sex with me in my chalet, and I froze – and not just because of the snow, the minus 30-degree weather, and the fact I had lost one of my gloves. Let's just say the evening didn't go as planned. I was so ashamed of my inability to have sex with this Frenchman that it was many, many years before I tried again. Oh God, I admit it. I was in my thirties. Oh dear God, how I wasted my twenties. I should have been backpacking round the world meeting boys, not sitting at home alone watching *thirtysomething* and trying to meet Jim Kerr.

Then, when at last I did have sex, yes, in my THIRTIES (the shame!), with Mad Richard, I did it quite a few times but that relationship only lasted six months. Then there was Trevor, and we only did if a few times because he couldn't stand the thought of a white girlfriend. And then there was Kevin, the Osama Bin Laden lookalike, and I think we only did it twice. Then, of course, there was my future, then current, and now ex, husband. We did it a lot at first, mostly during the exotic holidays

I whisked him away on, but as soon as we got married it sort of dribbled away. Even though we were married, I was still so shy, still so uncertain of his feelings towards me that I never once initiated sex between us, or even brought the subject up. I just made myself nice and clean and waxed in readiness. And so, in all the years I have been on this earth, I reckon I have had about two years' worth of normal sex. Add to that the fact I've never had a baby, and I might as well be just a blob, and not bother calling myself a woman at all. I'm like a nun who has never believed in God, i.e., pointless.

But, having said all that, the fact I was having hot, sweaty, loud sex with my husband (at the Aveda spa in Jamaica we actually shook spiders from their trees) didn't make me feel happier, or more attractive, or wanted, or loved. I felt more normal, as though I was doing what society expected me to do, but it didn't feel natural to me. I always felt I was acting a part, and maybe my husband could feel that. I am wondering whether I am going to give up the Hollywood waxes once and for all.

I walk back to the car and Michael sits on his towel and we drive slowly home. Michael senses my mood, and does his wolf shape.

CHAPTER 16

* * *

(In which a supermodel comes to stay)

It's a bright June day, and I plan to take Lizzie to her first horse show. Unfortunately, there's a supermodel in my spare bedroom. She's the sort of person I've bumped into over the years backstage at fashion shows and on shoots, but I wouldn't say she is a friend, more someone I 'mwah, mwah' every once in a while. While I had been talking to her backstage during London Fashion Week back in February, I had mentioned I no longer live in London, and in fact live on Exmoor. 'Near Patrick Cox?' she asked hopefully.

I never cease to be amazed by the fact vaguely famous or 'creative' people only acknowledge that places exist on the globe if another famous or 'creative' person has been there already. These people – Eurotrash, models, PRs – all seem to have a large circle of friends who are always inviting each other to 'the country' at the weekend. No one has ever invited me to stay with them in the country, ever. Okay, my ex-friend India once invited me to her New Year's Eve party in the Cotswolds, but I was made to sleep in a local pub and then when I tried to join everyone for breakfast the next day, I got lost and couldn't find the house again; I phoned her house but no one answered the telephone. Anyway, upon hearing that I have a farm, the model immediately invited herself down for the weekend. 'We could go to a pub!' she drawled (she is American; I think you could possibly prefix her name with the word 'super'). 'I love horses and riding, it's so good for the thighs!'

'Hmm, well, it's all a bit basic, I'm afraid, until I get the house done up. And Lizzie isn't really a normal horse yet. But I suppose we could walk the dog.'

'I have a dog!' she said suddenly, unzipping her Louis Vuitton. 'He's called David. See?'

Anyway, she continued to email me, telling me about all her various 'fuck buddies' in the fashion capitals of the world, saying she needed some 'down time'. So I had the brainwave of inviting her along on the weekend of the horse show, giving her a slice of good old English tradition. I thought she could, as a celebrity, open the proceedings. I admit I was slightly proud when I rang Penny, the organiser, to have a famous friend.

The horse and dog show is to be held at a beautiful house with parkland about two villages away. It is purely a show for rescued animals, and so I plan to parade Lizzie in hand, in all her finery. The day before the show, I felt as though I was in one of my pony books: sponging my Harry Hall hacking jacket, ironing my fawn tie. I planned to wash Lizzie's mane and tail, which is easier said than done, as she hates water. I used Frederic Fekkai shampoo and conditioner – 'I know him!' said the supermodel, standing in shorts and flip-flops about 50 feet away from Lizzie, sipping champagne and talking on her Black-Berry – and had to sponge Lizzie very, very gently, distracting her with a hay net and a completely silent calming CD. I groomed her until my arms ached, and polished her until she gleamed.

On the morning of the show, I get up at 6 am to resume my ministering. The night before I had taken the model to the local bistro. She had dressed down and wasn't wearing a scrap of make-up but still managed to look as though she had been sculpted from caramel; when I don't wear make-up, people ask me whether one of my cats has just died. I once went for a drink with a screenwriter who told me he likes women who just get out of bed in the morning, shake their mane of shiny hair, pull on a pair of jeans and a T-shirt, and are 'just a knockout. I call it the shower test. Never mind the artifice, you should look great straight out of the shower.' He should date this woman. She even makes my Hunter wellies look chic. When we walked into the bar, everyone fell silent, and all eyes swivelled in our (okay, her) direction. It was just like the moment when the two students go into a pub in *An American Werewolf in London*.

Lizzie, using the intuition she would have utilised in the wild to avoid coyotes and wolves, knows something is up and keeps looking round at me, deeply suspicious. I snap on the smart headcollar she wears only for best, put on a summer sheet that is blue gingham and very smart, and bandage her legs and tail. The horsebox arrives, and I lead her proudly to it. To my surprise, she walks straight up the ramp, and I tie her up. I shut the ramp, and run to fetch Michael, my bag, and the supermodel. As I run back to the box I can hear Lizzie. She is literally kicking the box down. Bang, bang, bang with her front legs. The driver looks alarmed. The box is rocking violently. 'She will have taken all the skin off her knees,' he says, and so I immediately lower the ramp. Lizzie is in a state, covered in sweat. Her knees are fine, but I cannot risk driving her anywhere. I untie her, and she immediately relaxes. I lead her down the ramp and back onto the yard where the ponies are standing, goggle-eyed and anxious. I realise Lizzie had thought I was about to get rid of her.

I thank the driver, who goes away, obviously thinking I am the most hopeless horsewoman he has ever come across. I go to the show anyway, feeling silly in my jodhpurs, with Michael in the front seat on the model's lap, trying desperately to get hold of David in the bag and have gay animal sex. We enter the class for best rescue dog over the age of five, and I feel a fool trotting round the arena with him, still clutching my Prada handbag. He wins first prize: a rosette and a packet of biscuits. I don't mention the evisceration of the sheep episode to the judge in case she disqualifies him. I buy him an ice-cream from a stall inside one of the marquees and we sit, breathing in a smell that can only be found in England: dog, pony, freshly mown grass, canvas. I feel like a child. This is the childhood I wanted, I think, and I wonder if I am already too old and too jaded to enjoy it. The model tells me she is going to join some friends in the Cotswolds. It starts to rain, and so we pack up and go home.

CHAPTER 17

* * *

(In which we take Lizzie on her first hack)

It's a hot weekend in July. The garden is full of lupins, golden rod, bunny rabbits (antirrhinums), great big bushes of hydrangea, purple columns of delphinium and the delicate strands of London Pride and strange floppy poppies.

The flowers make me think of childhood, of my mum knelt on a towel with a trowel. Brian has hung a few baskets of flowers prepared by his wife, Liz, in the yard: trailing geraniums, white and blue stuff I don't know the name of, but Lizzie just reached up and promptly ate them. I wonder if they're poisonous. It's so hot, I have to take Michael for his walk along the Exe Valley Way, a disused railway line where it's shaded, or wait until evening and take him down to the river, where he splashes, barking happily, in the clean, icy water.

I had thought looking after the horses would be easier in the summer: they would languish under trees, flicking their tails lazily. There would be no mud: Benji, with his white socks, was particularly prone to mud fever, when he would be covered in mud and develop, well, a fever; all winter I had to wash his legs with tea tree oil shampoo, dry them with one of my best towels and dust his legs with Keratex Mud Shield Powder. But in summer, there would be no rugs to change and hang up to dry in front of the Aga. No ice to break. No need for hay, as there is so much grass, despite the best efforts of the sheep. But no, oh dear me no.

Lizzie turns out to be allergic to flies. If she's bitten, she leaps in the air and develops a nasty lump. I've tried to spray her with fly repellent, but she's scared of the noise the can makes, and hates the smell; I, too, hate putting anything remotely toxic on her, but she even hates the smell of Neem oil. And so, instead, I have to cover her with a fly rug and place a fly mask over her head, including her ears; she now resembles a beekeeper. The ponies cannot be allowed to get fat, and so wear grazing muzzles; they resemble Leonardo DiCaprio in *The Man in the Iron Mask*; Benji has learned to get his off by banging it against a gate, while Dream has developed a sore from hers. I must think of an alternative way to stop them from eating too much: I'm thinking hypnosis, maybe, or making them read women's glossy magazines.

On Saturday morning Nic and I decide to take Lizzie for her first hack. I take my crash cap out of its cellophane, breathing in its delicious new smell. I realise I've come no further since I was five years old. I'm still alone with my hat. I'm still nervous about getting on a horse.

I tack Lizzie up, put on her boots and pump her up. I put on a breastplate, which should stop her saddle sliding back towards her tail if we go up any steep hills. Quincy and Nic are all ready: she is so relaxed, sitting with one hand on the pommel, chatting. I get on. Lizzie senses I'm nervous and she stiffens. Quincy moves away, and we follow. I hold onto the neck strap in case she bucks; all the horses I've ever ridden have bucked, or snatched the reins from my hands, jerking me forward onto the pommel. Why am I doing this, I ask myself, ducking low-hanging branches only just in time. Why can I never seem to be able to enjoy things that other people do: skiing, marriage, food, sex? To be honest, with my husband I found the anticipation of sex more exciting than the actual act. I always found it awkward when he slung my legs over his shoulder. I was always worried about what I looked like, what exactly was wobbling. Why couldn't I just lose myself in the moment? Why can't I do so now?

We go left and pad along the lane; then we turn right. Nic is chatting away and I'm worried about whether Lizzie's boots have come off, if her girth is too tight or too loose, will we meet a speeding car at the next bend, that sort of thing. We pass a pile of haylage bales, all wrapped in plastic, and Lizzie gives them a glare. A lone horse in a field spots us and starts galloping alongside. Lizzie turns her short, muscly neck to look, but otherwise does nothing. We startle a pheasant, which clatters away in our path, gets confused, and clatters past again. Lizzie blinks her Penélope Cruz eyes. We come across children on bicycles ('Why aren't they at home watching TV?' I ask Nic), and they whirr past us and Lizzie ignores them.

We've just turned a corner, and are between two such

high, dense hedges it's almost dark, a very green dark. I've started to relax, to let go of the neck strap and am looking, for the first time, at the view. Lizzie tenses very slightly; she has heard something in the field to her right, but she can't see what it is. All of a sudden, a gun explodes to our right, inches from Lizzie's head. For a split second, I think Lizzie's going to be okay. I feel her body coiled beneath me, like a rubber band; she seems to be vibrating on the spot. I notice Quincy's large bottom is right in front of us; even he is surprised by the noise, but is managing to control himself. I feel Lizzie trying to do the same, but finally she can control her fear no longer. I think the noise reminds her of the starting pistol of a race because now, finally – it feels like an age before she does what I know she is going to do, but the time span is only a few seconds – she launches herself forward. We shoot past Quincy and she's now at a gallop. I notice one of her boots flying off, and I crouch down, hanging onto the neck strap. I catch Nic saying something to me as we barrel past her, but I don't know what it is. 'Hang on!' probably. (I find out later she was swearing at the person who had let off the gun.) I know I mustn't fall off because if I do, there's no telling where Lizzie will end up. I know at the end of this lane is a bigger road, with two-way traffic. I read in my manual of horsemanship that if a horse bolts, the first few seconds are vital, you must try to turn the horse, rather than pulling on the reins. After the first few seconds, a horse goes into a sort of trance, unable to listen to anything, and will only stop once it hits something – a wall, a barbed-wire fence – or eventually runs out of steam.

I talk to Lizzie, and whisper 'Calm, calm' in her ear but she's not listening. If I wasn't so terrified, I would marvel at her smooth speed. I cannot turn her as the lane is so narrow, and I hope to God we don't meet anyone coming the other way. We reach a straight bit, and I know at the end is the road. I try to sit back, and pull on my light-as-air reins, but can do nothing. Maybe one minute has gone past. Then, ahead of me, I see a shape on the ground. It circles and it is black and white and I see that it's Michael. How has he got here? I had left him on the yard as I didn't want him to get under Lizzie's feet on her first outing into the big, bad world with me on board. He's agitated and barks frantically, doing a dance with his front paws. Lizzie's attention is diverted for a split second and miraculously she trots before we get to him. She stops and I slither off her back, shaking. Michael is wriggling. Nic and Quincy have trotted up to us. 'That dog!' she says, slightly out of breath. I say I think he had been following us, out of sight in the fields. 'You saved his life, he saved yours,' she says, and I think she might be right.

As I loosen the girth, which is caked in sweat, I notice a great big, angry wheal on Lizzie's stomach. She must have been bitten at some point, but even so, she hadn't done what she normally does, which is to put in a flying buck. She had been trying to look after me. Any horse would have reacted to a gun so close to its head. I wonder if it had been deliberate, given my outspoken anti-bloodsports stance, but shake that thought from my mind for the moment. We walk all the way home and, having done a loop over stone bridges and under canopies of trees, we reach the hill back to the farm.

As I walk alongside Lizzie, I thank her for trying to take care of me, for doing her best. She was only doing what she had been trained to do. I think of the words a psychic healer had once said to me. I had gone to see her during a particularly turbulent period in my marriage when I was imagining my husband with someone else's legs wrapped around his neck like a scarf. She told me she could see me, one day, living in a house on a hill surrounded by trees, with some sort of animal sanctuary. I told her I had just bought my perfect house in London and so that was never going to happen. I told her that I was worried my husband would abandon me, would fall in love with someone else. 'Whatever you brood over will hatch,' she had said to me wisely as I stood up to leave. If only I had paid more attention at the time.

I decide I'm going to visualise Lizzie being good, not me falling at her feet. I'm going to try to trust her just a little bit more. The very last New Year's Eve I spent with my husband we had told each other what resolution we would like the other to make. I had asked him to vow to 'be nicer to me'. He asked me to make a resolution that I would 'be more happy'. You can see from the resolutions we asked each other to make how I was the more needy, selfish one. I decide, as I place the saddle on its rack, that this is the day I will start to become more confident. That I should not feel the fear and do it anyway, but that I will not be afraid. That I will try, for the first time in my life, to be happy.

*

My friend Livia turns up one Saturday afternoon. She is en route to the coast, where she has rented a house on the beach for a few weeks, and has her husband, three, no, four children (her baby daughter is called Spangles) and a female lurcher called Bonnie in tow. Michael immediately mounts her (Bonnie, not Livia) and they get stuck together, end to end. It's so embarrassing. Her two oldest sons keep pointing at them and laughing. I make leek and potato soup; the problem is, while I have plenty of potatoes, I don't have any leeks, so it's all a bit brown and slimy. I had bought the potatoes from Emily, having gone up to the vegetable garden, Sweetie skipping at my heels, to reap something, but then realised I didn't know whether anything was ready. The broccoli had gone brown, the courgettes were in flower, so I thought eating them would be wrong in case having a flower is the plant equivalent of being pregnant, the tomatoes were still tiny, bullet-like yellow spheres, and the potatoes, well ... as they are underground, I've no idea what they're doing. If only they would give me some sort of sign.

Livia, who is always quite blunt, puts her spoon down. 'Don't you go a bit mad down here on your own?' she asks me. We go to sit on the lawn at the side of my house; the view is stunning, the smells all hot and summery, like a horticultural show but without the tents and ropes and the pressure to win a prize. I once dressed a wooden spoon in my Sindy doll's riding outfit; I didn't even get a Highly Commended, I think one of the judges murmured the word 'laziness', but it was an indication, I suppose, that at some point in the future, a very long way off, jodhpurs and smart black tailored jackets would loom large in my consciousness.

'I couldn't stand it,' Livia continues, drinking her tea and sipping in the view. It's odd, isn't it, how people feel perfectly at ease criticising your lifestyle, whereas can you imagine if you said to them, hmm, well, how can you bear to have four children? The noise! How do you work, what about your figure, isn't your house now a bit of a dump, what on earth do you spend a week on food? My friend Pip phoned the other day to ask how I was getting on and when I told him about the outdoor manège he said, 'Dear Lord, how on earth can you afford that?' This from a man with two homes (one is in the South of France), several buy-to-let flats and three children he put through private education. It's never, ever okay to say to someone, 'Four children! Never mind the cost to the environment, how on earth do you make ends meet?' But if you have animals and nice things just for you, then watch out because you're suddenly a prime target for all their latent fears and jealousies. People, I find, always want you to be just like them.

'I want to move,' Liv goes on. 'We have a pretty big garden, but nothing like this. It's a bit of a waste, isn't it, with just poor you [!].' I'm also finding that because I'm female and single, the general consensus in the area is that a) I can't possibly afford or deserve to live where I do. And b) I don't know what the hell I'm doing, viz people telling me which paddocks I should graze my horses in, trying to sell me ex-farm Land Rovers that don't even have any seats ('What am I supposed to do, crouch, install a cushion?' I asked the farmer when he showed it to me), that sort of thing.

'What on earth do you do at night?' Liv asks me. Note that I don't ask her this question. Note I don't say, 'Well, Livvy loo. How on earth can you ever go out with four children under 11? Aren't you just, well, plain exhausted once you've fed them all, done the washing, cleaned the house? Oh, I forgot, you don't clean it. You just allow your horrid batch to squirt milk into the sofa cushions. And aren't you worried about not losing that baby weight?' Instead I mumble that, well, I don't go out much, although in my defence I did go to a screening at Brompton Regis Town Hall the other Wednesday evening. We all sat on fold-up chairs under fluorescent strip lighting to watch *Mamma Mia!*. It was marvellous! I think to myself that, actually, I spend quite a lot of time, glass of white wine in hand, sat on the stone steps to the top paddock, listening to the horses moving in the grass, breathing in the scent of the sweet peas that are having a riot around my porch. No one to boss me. No one to phone me from upstairs to tell me to 'keep it down'. I start to think how lucky I am in my self-imposed solitude.

'Oh my God!' she suddenly exclaims, leaping out of her seat so quickly she sends it flying, noticing that 50 per cent of her children plus dog are missing. 'Have you got a pond! Where's Spangles!'

CHAPTER 18

* * *

(In which I find out my ex-husband is dating a pole dancer, while all I have to look forward to is a rerun episode of Follyfoot)

I'm in a taxi on Lower Regent Street in London, on my way to review the *Sex and the City* film. It makes me cry and think of my lost youth, the disappointment, the compromise, the betrayal, how we are all on a journey that can only end in a lonely death, which I'm sure isn't the reaction the makers will have wanted at all. My mobile goes. It's my ex-husband. He wants to meet for dinner. I fly into a panic, book a room I can no longer afford at the recently refurbished Connaught Hotel and an emergency knee wax and root retouch at Nicky Clarke over the road. I hare into Balenciaga, which is right next to the hotel. The shop seems impossibly shiny and clean; I used to feel so at home in places like this. Now, though, I feel old, tired, dirty and provincial, even though the sales assistant, desperate for her commission, tells me I look just like Jennifer Connelly. Yeah, I think, after she has lived through a nuclear winter.

I meet him in Eat and Two Veg, a vegetarian restaurant on Marylebone High Street. I spot him in the mirrors lining the walls as he approaches my table; he doesn't think I can see him yet, and is grinning from ear to ear. He adjusts his features into an expression more tantamount to nonchalance as he pulls out a chair. We eat. We go back to my hotel room. I order a film I don't want to watch on pay per view (one of the things I've appreciated since becoming single is being able to watch girly films rather than violent ones about superheroes). He lies on the giant bed and goes to sleep. Later, having spent a good few hours waiting for him to wake up, I start to fill out one of those cards you hang on the door for breakfast; this is my favourite part of staying in a hotel room, it's almost like writing a letter to Santa. He sits bolt upright. 'I'm not staying,' he says, going over to my laptop to check his emails. He goes into the bathroom to freshen up. I quickly, furtively, look at his inbox. There's one from someone who appears to be his new girlfriend. She's being hysterical and demanding. 'Just because you lent me some money doesn't mean you own me!' she has typed. She seems much more difficult and proprietorial than I was, and we were married! And then I see that a few emails later he has typed those three words: 'I love you.'

As he leaves, he asks if I have any change for his taxi. I say that he can look in my bag. He takes £20 out of my wallet and closes the door, whistling softly.

When I get home to Somerset the next morning, I Google the name of his girlfriend. It turns out she recently wrote a blog about her new 'British-born Sikh boyfriend', saying how much she loves Asian 'boys', and how cool her new boyfriend is because he doesn't look at the colour of a woman's skin when choosing a partner, he just 'checks out her arse'. He interjects in this 'article' (while my ex-husband hated me writing about him in my newspaper column, perhaps he doesn't mind her blogging about him because NOBODY WILL EVER READ IT) that he's happy in his new 'relationship' because 'having gone through a divorce, I'm not about to marry a nice Indian girl'.

It turns out she is five years younger than he is (!), went to Cambridge (!), worked her way around the world and has written a book about her several years spent working in Manhattan as a stripper and pole dancer (an infinite number of !!!!!!). She has her own website, on which you can read all the reviews of said book (only the good ones, naturally), and watch a slide show of her kneeling on a bed in her New York apartment dressed only in a G-string, or draped around a pole, mouth open provocatively. Oh, and she also teaches Ashtanga yoga. This is obviously his ideal woman: brainy, young, works in the sex industry, bendy, lives in a different country so that he gets his all-important 'space'. Not that brainy, though. Slumming it in the sex industry because you think you're being ironic and post-modern, when in fact you are insulting the women who are forced into it because of exploitation, addiction, trafficking or real poverty, is pretty damn stupid, and sick.

To be honest I feel quite sick when I start reading more about her. Not because of the pornographic content of her book or her website, but because I realise how very far removed I was, and am, and will ever be, from what my husband, what any man, really wants in a woman. Oh my godfathers, how far I am: whereas I used to worry that finely milled face powder might settle in the fine lines around my eyes, now I worry about ingrained dirt doing the same thing. I didn't notice there was a bramble stuck in my hair until Emily carefully, tactfully, reached up to remove it when I popped into her shop to shelter from the rain; I was very lucky it hadn't put down roots. Even when we were married, I hated phoning him; I would think, 'He doesn't want to hear from me, I might be interrupting him.' I'm reserved, inhibited, physically flawed, stupid, old.

Maybe I should have been more difficult, more demanding, screamed more for his attention rather than retreating, trying not to bother him, sending him off to places so that he could find himself. What self-respecting woman does that? I can just picture his smug, fat face in bed with this compulsively exhibitionist young lady. That evening in the hotel room at the Connaught, when he wasn't sleeping or raiding the mini-bar for sweets, he had been dying to tell me something. 'I have something amazing to tell you,' he smirked, 'but I can't because you'll write about it.'

What is puzzling me is not how on earth he could go out with a pole dancer, but how on earth do these men, no matter that they are lazy, mean with money and living with their mums, manage to persuade fairly good-looking (although rather short, with chubby thighs), educated (if deluded) women to go out with them? Why is he living out his fantasies while all I have to look forward to this weekend is a rerun episode of *Follyfoot*? Growing up, oh how I yearned to be Dora, with her feather-cut hair and her horses and her crush on the dark-haired Steve. Should we all be posting pictures of our naked buttocks on the internet? Why does she deserve to be loved and not me?

The next day, I sit down at my computer trying to get warm (it might be high summer, but it's still freakishly cold in the house) from its weak glow. There is an email from him sitting in my inbox ominously entitled 'US'. Us, Us? There was never an Us, even when we were married. I open it, heart beating. Perhaps he has seen the error of his ways and wants to win me back. But no.

'I have to come clean and admit I've been seeing someone. It's a new relationship and I don't know where it's going, but I didn't tell you because I didn't want you to write about her. I said I was single in order to protect her. I should not have come to see you, despite there being no sexual contact between us. It's not fair on you, her, or myself. Neither you nor I will ever move on as long as I don't face up to my fear of losing you as a friend [!], knowing that it would be even more final than the divorce. I've used you as a crutch – someone to call and see when I've had difficult times with her, when really I should have been addressing my issues directly with her.

'I need to grow up. I would like us to stay friends, but I need to start telling you what's happening in my life. I was wrong to hang out in your hotel with you and hug you while seeing her. I hope we can be mature and deal with our new reality as platonic friends. I would love to see you again before I go to India, but when I leave I need to focus on becoming an independent person and getting over our marriage – the end of which I'm still mourning. I know that you're still in love with me [!] but we need to accept that we should change that love to a friendship that will last for ever. I'm with someone now but have no idea if it will last. I'm telling you in order to face my fears, stop being selfish and grow up and take responsibility for myself. You are a beautiful and intelligent woman and you need to move on, too. I hope you understand . . .'

At first I think, hmm, that's quite nice, and I sent him this: 'N, that's OK. I assumed you have a girlfriend, why wouldn't you? You had plenty while we were married. You talk about not being fair on her by just having a drink with someone you knew for seven years; what about being fair on me and having sex behind my back with some trollop you had just met? [You can see I become more irate as the email goes along.] If she felt jealous and betrayed after just a few months, can you imagine how I felt when I found out about Daphne et al? Perhaps now you realise what I went through. It was wrong of you to stay with me for so long when you had no intention of being faithful. I guarantee that if you mess this woman around she will write about you, probably in a graphic way. Anyway, a real live pole dancer. You must be very happy.'

Then I read his email again, and became angrier and angrier at the injustice of it all, and so I sent him another one:

'"In order to protect her?" It would have been nice if

you had protected me. I hope she cheats on you several years into a "marriage", perhaps after you have funded her second sordid "book". BTW, you owe me £6,000 for the divorce costs, which the court ordered you pay, plus the £20 you took out of my wallet in the hotel. Can you put both in the post today rather than giving money to a woman you've just met? I assume you just fold bills and put them directly into her knickers. L'

I felt better after I had sent that, but then gloom descended. As I pulled on my woolly hat and struggled into my wellies on the doorstep, I wished with all my heart that I lived in a New York apartment, was young, was demanding and thrilling and had a boyfriend who had just typed those three words: 'I love you.'

CHAPTER 19

* * *

(In which I feel as though I'm living in a nativity play)

I didn't finish telling you the hideous life cycle of the sheep. In early spring, the pregnant ewes give birth, and there is a delicious time when lambs frolic beneath their bellies: shy, playful, full of joy. Fearful that he would be shot red-pawed with a lamb poised accusingly between his jaws, I'd been forced to make Michael wear a muzzle, which he hated, until one day I just sat him down and reasoned with him, and asked him to stop chasing the sheep. I took his muzzle off for our morning walk, and from that day on he has shown no interest in wanting to chase sheep or eviscerate them. I think he has learned to listen to reason. Anyway, as soon as the lambs reach about 10 months of age, Patrick the farmer takes them away. 'Where are the lambs going?' I ask him. It turns out they are going to slaughter. The mothers are literally wrenched from their babies, then impregnated a few weeks later (artificially, I might wager; why give them a moment of brief, natural happiness?) and the whole blasted business starts all over again.

I ask the farmer what happens to the wool that's shorn in the summer. It's burnt, apparently, as it's worthless. Either that or it's buried. These sheep are just meat animals. Over time, they have been bred to be bigger and bigger, which means the dogs that control them have to be fiercer, too. Eventually, many of the dogs become so large and aggressive that their teeth have to be removed. I recently passed a flock of sheep on the lane being driven to a new field by a pair of collies who were so ferocious, so impatient, the sheep were literally falling over themselves to get away from them; one scrambled across the bonnet of my car, scratching it. This can't be right. So it wasn't Michael's fault he was being so overzealous; it was in his genes. He was punished for behaving that way, nonetheless.

I ask the farmer if I can keep just one of the sheep, whom I have christened Marge (she has a tall, teetering beehive of wool on her head, like her cartoon namesake). She has twins, and no matter how many times the farmer put her back with the others in the big field, she and her twins would escape, Steve McQueen-fashion, under the barbed wire and hide out in the orchard. 'You'll be phoning me every five minutes with a problem,' he says. 'She's a bolter. She needs to be shot.' 'No, I won't call you up about them, ever. I want Marge and the twins. I'm not asking you to give them to me. I will pay the market price for them, whatever that is.'

On Sunday I wake up and it's eerily quiet. I look out my window. All the sheep have gone. Oh no. I race down the stairs, fling open the back door and shove my feet into my wellies, tucking in my pyjamas, and hare to the orchard. It too is empty. Marge and the twins have gone.

It's very harsh here in the countryside. Even on a Sunday, supposedly God's day of rest, all I can hear is the pop, pop, pop of someone shooting something; I could almost be living in Hackney. I wonder how people can call this sort of activity a blood sport. What sort of sport is it if one of you has a shotgun, and your opponent has fur or feathers and is without an opposable thumb? I'm sitting at my kitchen table, grieving over the fact the lambs have by now probably met a horrible death, when I get a phone call. It's from my friend Isobel. She, like me, left London to live the rural idyll; she chose to settle on the Yorkshire Moors. Also like me, she has a dog (in her case, a black female Labrador) but no man in her life, and precious few friends. I have started to wonder where all my friends have gone, actually. I should place them on the endangered species list, along with red kites, Exmoor ponies, dormice and otters. All of these elusive creatures seem to thrive not inches from my door − I saw an otter in the river near the Tarr Steps (a prehistoric bridge of stones placed across the River Barle in about 1000 BC) a few weeks ago, cruising on her back, whiskers bejewelled − but my friends seem to have met the same fate as red squirrels. (I love the grey squirrels who play outside the hay barn. There was a lone male for quite a long time, who seemed to be quite bored and frustrated − I half expected him to start drinking Red Stripe and leave behind a pile of crumpled cans – and then suddenly he found a female and they had babies, mini squirrels who eat all the grapes on my vine. Such a fuss is made of the fact that the greys are not indigenous wildlife, but neither are the birds who just come here on holiday, the migrants, the ones with second homes.) I recently emailed the man who had been my, sort of, best man, and he sent a curt, businesslike reply, and signed his missive, 'Best.' That's almost as bad as your husband ending a phone call when you are in an earthquake zone and he is ON HOLIDAY with the immortal, meaningless words, 'You take care.' I think the reason my best man is no longer my friend is that I must have bored him silly moaning about my husband and then not followed his advice. But then I guess loads of women do that, don't they? Was I any worse than the rest?

Isobel owns a herd of about 300 Shetland and Wensleydale ('I thought that was just a crumbly cheese,' I say to her stupidly) sheep, from which she spins ethical wool. She tells me of a woman, quite near me on the moor, who has three halter-trained Shetland lambs she had bred for showing, but as they are now getting beyond the cute stage she is about to take them for slaughter. Like me and Nicola, Isobel now feels she hates people. In London, I would always get annoyed at the casual rudeness of people, who would make obscene gestures if you failed to zoom off at 100 miles per hour at a green light, who would push you aside to get onto the Tube, but here in deepest rural England the callousness and thirst for blood is so completely in your face it's hard to ignore. Everywhere you turn there are gun shops and still pools of lakes with signs next to them advertising fly fishing. At the end of every lane to a farm is invariably a sign, depending on the time of year, for 'home-killed lamb', 'hung pheasant' or 'brown-feathered turkey'. I once had a heated argument with the male sports editor of my newspaper who remarked dimly that if it weren't for farming and people eating meat, cows, pigs and sheep would not exist. I told him that that wasn't even an argument. That it would be far better not to impregnate a sheep so that she gives birth to a lamb which is killed before it's a year old. It would be far better if a sheep were not to exist, rather than be made pregnant again and again and again before having its throat slit. I wonder if people who eat lamb have seen a mother, like I saw Marge when she was returned to my land pregnant, searching for her lost lambs, calling for them desperately. How much better to never have lived rather than to be subjected to grief and loss you don't understand, over and over again. It's like my mum, suffering from dementia. One of my sisters told her that my nephew has leukaemia. Tears flowed from my mum's tiny blue eyes. She would then forget she had ever been told. My sister told her again. She heard the news and felt the grief afresh, as if for the first time.

Isobel wonders if I'm able to take in the lambs, who are named Caitlin, Willow and Ash. She promises she will send me an email, telling me how to look after them. I'm slightly worried that Michael will eat them, but I don't tell her this and instead I say, 'Yes, of course I will have them.' How could I say no?

The sheep woman arrives with a small trailer on the back of a smart 4x4. She seems quite normal, not at all like a person who would slaughter halter-trained pets who are only six months old. She gives me a form from Defra to fill in. I refuse to do so – I remember, when working on the *Evening Standard*, we had sent two sheep to the TV critic, who was then living in the Black Mountains of Wales. He fell in love with them. They became his surrogate children, better than children, and then when the foot and mouth crisis struck in 2001 he had had to surrender them for slaughter.

I'm not going to allow that to happen to my lambs. I pick up a scoop full of horse nuts and the sheep follow me: they are tiny, brown and cream balls of wool, their legs like knitting needles sticking out at odd angles. I show them to their quarters: a stone hut, more a loft really, in the orchard; I had, at very short notice, evicted Brian's (Brain's) gardening tools.

The lambs follow me everywhere, bleating. I feel I should be wearing a smock and bonnet and be carrying a crook. Michael circles them, crouching low in the grass, all his skills coming back to him. When he gets too close, Caitlin headbutts him, showing a great deal of self-esteem and chutzpah, probably from her brief spell as a beauty contestant, and I know they will be safe with him, that they are able to put him in his place. I love my lambies.

I wonder at people who say sheep are stupid, that people

'follow like sheep', or are like 'a lamb to the slaughter'. These creatures are intelligent, adventurous (they keep climbing over the hedges to get to me, using each other as stepping stones) and naughty; Caitlin gallops at me, head down, to batter me with her horns if I'm slow with her supper. The sheep woman beats a hasty retreat; I wonder she isn't ashamed. 'I didn't want to send them to auction, to be moved from pillar to post, so I thought it best to send them to slaughter locally,' she says as she backs her vehicle out onto the lane. I don't even bother to ask why on earth she didn't just keep them. Animals these days are as disposable as a £9 cashmere sweater from Primark.

Isobel sends a text to ask if the lambs are okay, offering to pick them up to join her flock in Yorkshire when she can. She never breeds from her sheep, acquiring more by mopping up those destined for the chop. Apparently, she tells me, sheep can live into their twenties. The problem is, no one knows exactly how long they will live and give us wool (Shetland wool is the finest and the warmest in the world, a million times better than imported Australian merino), because no flock has ever been allowed to live out its natural lifespan. I lean over the orchard fence, watching my lambs exploring their new home. I dial Isobel's number. 'Hi,' I say. 'They're here! And I've decided to keep them.'

Wanting to give the lambies some space, I wander down the field to fetch Lizzie in. She peels away from the others and I take off her fly mask. I notice her left eye is watering and I wonder if a fly has got in under the mask. Her eyes have never been quite right since I got her, something I put down to her having hay chucked over her head at the livery yard, so the seeds went in her eyes. Although she's still quite head-shy, jerking away from me if I so much as reach up to her (a sure sign that she was once struck around the head), I have tried, with limited success, to clean her eyes each day with a cotton wool pad soaked in Optrex. I had thought they were getting better, but today I can see her left eye is red and puffy, as if she was out late last night drinking Chardonnay. I call Simon the vet; I think by now he reckons I've got Munchausen's Syndrome, but he agrees to call in later that day.

I put Lizzie in her stable, which she hates, battering the door with her front legs, doing mad circles that tangle the straw into a whorl. When Simon arrives, he peers into Lizzie's eye. 'Hmm.' He gives her a sedative, then applies some green dye to her cornea. She does look odd. He peers some more. Despite the fact she's so wobbly on her feet that she resembles Bambi, she tries to eat him. At long last he can see what the problem is: the blunt end of a thorn. It has pierced her eyeball. He can't get it out. 'How did that happen with her face mask on?' I ask. 'It's easily done. She must've been trying to eat something in the hedge. I have to take her into the clinic, I'm afraid. The worst-case scenario is that it will become infected, and she will lose her eye.'

And so the next morning I hire a box and driver and, after Lizzie climbed on board quite readily, she realised she was going and started to batter the inside of the box with her hooves, we set off to the clinic, not too far away across the border in Devon. We take Dream along for the ride, to keep Lizzie company. When we arrive Lizzie stampedes off the ramp, me trailing behind her (she does so love to show me up) and is installed in a lovely clean box with cardboard as a bed, with Dream looking small next door. I have to wait two hours for the specialist to arrive. When he does, we lead Lizzie into a darkened, padded operating room. She looks as if she has been crying; perhaps she has. She has been sedated again, more heavily this time, and can barely stand. I'm told to go and sit in the waiting room. After another excruciating wait, during which I read leaflets on all sorts of awful diseases I now imagine all of my animals to be suffering from, the specialist comes in, a light on his head above a huge smile. 'We got it out!' he says triumphantly. 'She will have to remain here under observation for a couple of days, and be on antibiotics to ensure there's no infection, but she'll be as right as rain. She'll have a tiny scar on the front of her eye, though.'

'Never mind, Lizzie,' I say to her through the bars of her stable, watching her anxiously as she begins to come round. I go in and kiss her muzzle, taking liberties, doing all the things I want to do to her (I particularly love gently pulling her large ears) but cannot because she's too fierce and combative. A tube has been stitched to her face, entering the corner of her eye through a tear duct, drip drip dripping antibiotics onto her eye; the nurse had decided my horse is too head-shy to tolerate having drops applied every hour, and hopefully will find this method less stressful. She looks in a terrible state. Dream's big bouffant is trying to look over the dividing wall. 'None of us is perfect,' I tell them. 'That doesn't mean you don't deserve to be loved.'

CHAPTER 20

* * *

(In which I realise I'm as old as Madonna, although not quite as honed)

It's September. It's my 50th birthday. I am officially old. Unlovable. I might be the same age as Madonna but I don't have her facilities. I know now I will never, ever have children. I suppose if I'd really wanted a child, I could've made it happen. Maybe, when you're five years old, your whole future is mapped out for you. While my sister had a doll called Simon, a horrid pink, fat thing with gingham drawers, I had those tiny plastic horses and a show-jumping white rabbit. The only outfit I ever bought for my 1960s Sindy, who came in her box already dressed in chambray jeans and a striped sweater, was a pair of jodhpurs and a riding hat that refused, rather annoyingly, to fit over her blonde hairdo. Rather than asking to be given her boyfriend, Paul, or her little sister, Patch, for my ninth birthday, I asked for the horse, but was told it was too expensive. I longed for the mini grooming kit (curry comb, broom, tiny trophy) rather than the hair-styling kit (heated rollers, a mirror, a towel, brushes with S-shaped handles) or the Let's Go to the Beach kit (parasol, sunglasses, an orange cooler and yellow swimsuit).

I'm in a hotel room at the Mercer in SoHo, New York. It has an impressive lobby lined with books nobody ever reads as they're too busy looking over the head of the person they're with in the hope of glimpsing someone famous, or at least thinner and more expensively dressed. The rooms are the size of a ladies' hanky. It has very unfriendly mirrors to make the room seem bigger that I have to slide past, lights turned low in case I catch a glimpse of myself. You remember how my husband said that my issues started long before he met me? He was certainly right about that. Even at school, I would creep along the side of the cloakroom so that I wouldn't have to see myself in the mirror and would wash my hands in the sink at an awkward angle. I remember one Christmas my mum bought me a No 7 gift box that contained foundation. I discovered that with a thick layer of foundation on, I could, for the very first time, look at my face in the mirror. These halcyon years of self-acceptance and optimism that one day David Cassidy or Ben Murphy (oh dear God, I've just, sadly, looked him up on the *Alias Smith and Jones* website and discovered he is 65!) might just turn up unannounced and ask me on a date to the cinema continued for quite a few years, until I discovered I had become hopelessly short-sighted (I was in my mid-twenties, having driving lessons, and kept alarming the instructor by nearly mowing down pedestrians). Putting on glasses, and seeing my face for what it truly was, scarred me deeply. I think I preferred being blind, in a delicious blur where I could delude myself that I looked exactly like that girl in the Sarah Moon Biba ad.

How could I have expected anyone to love me when I didn't want anyone, including myself, to so much as look at me? I've had one strange encounter with a boring man since moving to Exmoor, not including when my ex-husband came for New Year's Eve. A male reader had emailed me to say the photo of me taken in Ethiopia with a donkey (I had written in my newspaper about the trip to Africa to see the work the Brooke charity does in developing countries with horses, mules and donkeys; the trip broke my heart) and as he sounded nice on email, and wrote eloquently about his ginger cat (he would climb up the flock wallpaper of his house like a gekko; the cat, not the man), I agreed to meet him for a drink, sight unseen. I dressed up in Alaïa and got the mud out from under my fingernails. I looked nice; well, I looked clean, at least. I met him in the bar of Claridge's. It was so nice to be somewhere all twinkly and warm and clean. He was already in a booth sitting down. He stood up. There was very little difference. (I wonder why men are no longer tall. Or is it that women just wear higher and higher heels?) Wanting to keep the conversation as far away from anything saucy as I possibly could, I started telling him about the horses. 'Hmm,' he said, nodding wisely, like men do. I have never yet come across a man who will admit to not knowing something about anything. I'm sure if I'd said I'd taken up potholing in the Andes at the weekend, this little man would've been down there first.

'Oh, I could ride her. I can ride anything,' he said. I chose to ignore that remark, thinking, I'm never bloody well letting you near either of us, and told him I was worried about her biting. 'I'd just give her a whack,' he said, demonstrating with his arm the range of motion required. I almost punched him. I started doing my bored demeanour (yawning, rummaging in my bag, picturing my pyjamas in my head, that sort of thing) and he got the hint and asked for the bill.

He texted me madly after that, saying that if I wanted to see him again he would be there 'like a shot'. He wrote in an email that he had often wondered why on earth I'm still single, but having met me realised that 'you know your worth. If I had known you looked like that in the flesh, I wouldn't have had the nerve to show up. The reason you are still single is that you haven't met anyone who measures up to you.' I tried to let him down gently (he was, after all, better looking than the man in the horsefeed place who's taken a bit of a shine to me – well, he carried the sacks of Fast Fibre to the boot of my car – but ultimately I couldn't get over the fact he looked like, and had the hand gestures of, Ken Dodd) over the next few days, but unfortunately he became rather angry. He wrote me an email, which he then posted on the internet (that was a nice touch, a touch that will, in all probability, survive even longer into infinity than the Tarr Steps), telling me that my upper lip was red and sore from waxing, and that in my purple Burberry platforms I had found it so difficult to walk that being with me was like 'helping an old lady across the road'. After that exchange, I felt a little bit pleased I'd retired from the race, gone into hibernation, sworn off men for life. Isn't dating a ridiculous dance that turns from gentle jousting and flirting to the exchange of bile in the blink of an eye?

I wonder if this is partly, if not wholly, the reason I love animals so much; maybe I'm not as selfless as I like to make out. Squeaky never recoils in the morning at my unadorned face. If she puts her paw on my tummy, I know she isn't thinking, hmm, now that feels a bit squidgy. Having Michael in my life has made me realise that I'm not a frigid person at all, that I am, in fact, quite spontaneous and tactile. Every morning I can't wait to hug him; his face lights up when he spots me in my pyjamas. I'm always taking his face in my hands and kissing him on his wet black nose. At night on the sofa I'm always holding his snowy white paws; to his credit, he doesn't snatch them away. I have, it seems, lots of love to give, but never before have I felt completely safe to do so. I guess the reason I was never effusive with my husband, or with anyone for that matter, even my mum, was that I feared rejection. Does it all boil down to how you were treated as a child? My mum was quite no-nonsense, unsentimental, practical, while my dad was, I think, quite shy. So between them they never once told me I was beautiful, or how special I was. Even if it had been a lie, it would've been nice to hear and believe for a bit.

My husband used to ask me what had triggered the anorexia in my early teens, and although I didn't know the answer to his question at the time, I now think that it took hold of me because I was never made to feel good enough. I think all my parents wanted was for me to survive childhood without being run over. (To this day, I get really scared crossing the road; I stand on the kerb, not daring to move until the running green man appears. In Delhi, faced with all the chaos and the rickshaws, I was paralysed with fear.) My parents never encouraged me to aim high; they just wanted me to be safe. The first and last time my dad told me I looked lovely, and was well dressed, was when he was lying in bed in hospital, a few weeks before he died. I suppose he felt he was running out of time to tell me what he should've told me all along: that I deserve love, that I have nothing to fear from life.

Let's face it, now that I live in a mouldering ruin, far, far, far from shops, and even further removed from beauty spas, I've had to confront who I really am, what on earth I have to offer. Anyway, what ridiculous places beauty spas are, aren't they? All this modern-day urging of women to be 'pampered', when in fact all it means is we face more pressure, more expense, more demands on our time, and still emerge looking exactly the same. I remember having a massage at some alternative place in Camden, and the male therapist saying to me that I seemed unhappy, was storing all these toxins in my shoulder muscles, that I should say a 17-word mantra twice a day and eliminate wheat from my diet. I told him he was supposed to make me feel less stressed, not more. All that stuff, all those clothes, all that perfection, all those props, all those diversions, was just an elaborate ruse to detract attention away from me, what I look like, how I always fall so desperately short. Looking back, I think the reason my husband didn't love me enough (because sometimes I do think he loved me, just a little bit) was because I didn't allow him to. His great big shining eyes were a mirror for my flaws. I was quite glad when he stopped looking at me.

I'm in New York for fashion week. The hotel is slap-bang opposite the Prada store, a few doors down from Marni and Marc Jacobs, but I can no longer afford designer clothes: all my money goes on vets, organic feed bills, various bits of tack, running repairs on the lawn-mower and the strimmer, that sort of thing. I used to be so glamorous. I don't care too much, not really. I used to nurse a weird ambition to own a bag from each and every Prada collection, a desire, I can see now, that is as shallow as my lake. I once spent £3,500 on a black cashmere coat from Jil Sander that wasn't even lined. I mean, what was I thinking? I have begun to realise now that fashion is a lie. You only have to look at the models leaving a show, dressed in torn jeans and flip flops, to realise that not only do they look far more beautiful, and far younger, without all the artifice, that even they would not spend all their money on designer clothes. They spend it on sensible things like real estate, and champagne, and exotic holidays.

I wake up on my birthday morning in the huge bed and check my BlackBerry. There is only one email, about work. A bunch of flowers is brought to my room along with my pot of black coffee. I perk up a bit, but the card says they're from a fashion designer. Ooh, it's a text. I spill my coffee on the white bed sheets. 'Happy birthday Liz. I sent some flowers to the farm but they said there was a storm and they couldn't get there until tomorrow as the road is blocked by fallen trees. N x'

Who on earth is N? And then I realise. It's my ex-husband. I don't have the heart to tell him I'm in New York and won't see the flowers when they finally arrive (despite seven years together, he never could get the dates of fashion week quite right). I text him thank you. I realise I no longer think about him all the time or expect to hear from him. I then get an email from Nicola. She tells me what the horses have been doing ('Lizzie is in a very good mood, has had all her feet scrubbed!'), how Michael and the cats are, how many eggs have been laid, whether the lambs still smell like wet jumpers, and I feel homesick all of a sudden. Why do I always want to be where I am not?

When I sit at a show later that morning, in a draughty concrete warehouse in Greenwich Village, two women talk around my body (I quite often think I'm invisible: at airport check-in lecterns, standing in Marni, sat in the lobby of my smart hotel) about their children and their awful, disobedient, sex-obsessed young nannies. Every now and then, they bark down the phone at their husbands. 'What do you mean you can't cope?' one of them says, irritated; she has Bluetooth connected, so for a moment I think she is barking at me, and I cower instinctively. 'How hard can it be? You just . . .' and she rattles off a list of instructions that are detailed enough to have landed Apollo 13. Sometimes, just occasionally, I'm glad I'm not normal. I would like to be warmer, and have more sleep, but I don't miss sharing a house with a monosyllabic nightmare. I don't care that I no longer have the latest Louis Vuitton graffiti bag. I might have loved all those things, but they never loved me back. I wonder how many of these women's husbands are, right now, having animal sex with someone as hairless as a billiard ball and as bendy as a yogi. At least that's one thing I no longer have to type into the list of problems I have neatly stored on my BlackBerry memo pad.

When I land a week later at Bristol Airport, I feel a bit sad that I'm the only person waiting by the conveyor belt for a suitcase who doesn't get a call on their mobile phone: it seems even really misshapen people in tracksuits are more popular than poor me. But, honestly, is it really worth being in a relationship just so you have someone who calls to see if you've landed? My husband used to do that, but in retrospect he was probably just checking what time I would be home, frantically changing the sheets and taking a shower before I arrived. Even when I can't quite locate where I left my car in the car park, I sigh with relief that there is no one with me to moan at my stupidity, dragging his feet like a toddler being taken to the dentist. The best thing about being on my own is that I can make mistakes.

I get home and can see straight away that Snoopy is ill. He's doing his teapot impression in the spare 'bathroom'.

I run my hands along his back and all I can feel is the bones of his spine. Nic, who's been looking after him, is beside herself. He has stopped eating, and when he goes to have a drink of water his head just drops in his bowl, so he almost drowns. She has been syringing chicken broth into his tiny mouth; as he is too weak to wash, he has crusty food all around his face. I can't lose Snoopy. I can't. I feel that without him, there will be one fewer being in the world who loves me. Selfish, I know. I email my ex-husband. Only he will know what I'm going through. It was he who, after all, taught Snoopy to put his tiny forehead forward for a kiss, something he's still doing, no matter he is so weak. 'He has been such a good friend to you,' my ex-husband writes back. 'Don't let him down.' I'm not going to let him down, I think to myself. I take him to a vet. The vet, a man with dirty fingernails, grabs Snoopy roughly by the scruff of his neck (being so thin and dehydrated, he doesn't have that much scruff), and tries to stick a thermometer up his bottom. Snoopy squirms round to tell him to stop it, his mouth open in a silent miaow. The vet's being so rough I grab his wrist and tell him to stop. He looks surprised. 'This cat isn't seriously ill,' he says. 'I think it's just toothache.' He injects him with painkiller and some antibiotics.

It seems vets in the countryside only take animals seriously if they're big, and black and white or pink, and people can potentially eat them. I take Snoopy home. He's listless. I gently syringe a broth of puréed chicken broth down his pink throat. The broth wasn't made from one of my chickens, I might add, although I forgot to tell you that I lost one, Gwen. She never quite recovered from the trauma of the battery farm and despite my best efforts and several courses of antibiotics she died one morning just before the weather got warmer – I had so wanted her to feel the sun on her small, speckled back just once. I buried her in the orchard and planted wild flowers on her grave and was mortified a few weeks later when Michael dug her up, ate her, and then vomited her up on the lawn. 'Don't eat our relatives!' I'd shouted at him.

I stay up with Snoopy all night, feeding him every two hours. I wake up once to hear the name tag on his collar tinkling against his water bowl, so I know he was managing to drink on his own. I don't expect him to pull through but, the next morning when I have dozed off, I feel him gently headbutting me.

A few days later I get in touch with a holistic vet called Jasper ('proper vet crumpet' Nic had told me) who has a practice in Bristol. He motors over one afternoon (Nic puts on pink eyeshadow and a sparkly knit beret, worn at a jaunty angle), and after examining Snoopy as gently as if he were a prized heirloom on *Antiques Roadshow*, he says he thinks it could be kidney failure. He takes some blood, and a few days later calls me to confirm the bad news. 'It is kidney failure,' he says, and although I hate what he is telling me, I still like the sound of his voice. 'He will never get better, but we can give him a better quality of life until he decides he is ready to leave you.'

If this was fiction, I would now be writing about how the vet stirred something in my loins, how our eyes met across the tiny patient, and he held my hand as he gave me the bad news. But I'm sorry to say I didn't fancy him: he was a bit too ginger and posh and Prince Harry like for my taste, with greasy hair. I also think that if a man manages to reach the age of 40 and not be married, gay or living with someone, there must be something badly wrong with him. Perhaps he has two false legs under his tweed trousers. He did phone me one Sunday morning, ostensibly to ask after Snoopy, but I could tell something else was on his mind. Who, I remember thinking, phones on a Sunday to ask about your cat? I was warm and friendly, and grateful, and told him I would keep him up to date with Snoopy's progress, and perhaps he could come out to see Snoopy again in a few weeks' time? He agreed, and I walked around that afternoon with a warm glow in my tummy, a spring in my wellingtons. How cruelly we can be let down, though. A few days later, I got his enormous bill, with a weekend phone consultation fee tacked on the end.

Ah well. I always seem to end up by paying for male attention, whereas other women get taken out to dinner, bought expensive jewellery, and taken on holiday and out for treats. *Private Eye* once wrote a piece saying I had divorced my husband because he only spent £300 on a pair of diamond earrings for my Christmas present. While technically true, they didn't take into account the years when he had given me a DVD of *Lost*, a programme I hadn't even liked, let alone understood, and an orchid in a horrid pot paid for with my credit card. My husband never once surprised me by meeting me from work and whisking me out to dinner. I wish I was more like those women who date men just so they will move a block of solidified concrete from the front of their house, give them sperm, that sort of thing. I have to admit I did once or twice steal my husband's sperm. Having first of all told me he didn't want children, he then decided he 'needed to be a dad', and then decided that, after all, he was too young to be a father and it would hinder him in his novel-writing, so he stopped having sex with me. So, one night, after giving him a hand job (as Samantha in *Sex and the City* quite rightly pointed out, a hand job is called that for a reason – it's hard work), I popped into the bathroom and inserted my slime-covered hand into my nether regions. It was all to no avail, of course (we know already that my ovaries had long-since retired to sit in deckchairs and read *Woman's Realm*) and I don't regret it now. What an unfair way to have a child. How could I have possibly taught it about love?

I don't feel dissatisfied with my choices. If I'd really wanted a baby I would've discussed that need with my husband before we got married, given that I was so much older than him. I often blame him, in my head and out loud, to anyone who will listen, for stealing my last child-bearing years but, in all honesty, he didn't steal them. I gave them to him. Rather than just vaguely hoping, half wishing, that I would get pregnant during our first couple of years together (we never once used contraception; I thought at the time this meant that he was happy to have a child with me or at least not totally averse to the idea, but with the benefit of hindsight I have come to the realisation he simply assumed I was past it), I could've got myself checked out, had some tests run, that sort of thing. About a year before we split up I discovered for many years I'd had endometriosis, a scarring of the Fallopian tubes that would have made conception difficult, no matter my age. It was fixable, but of course, as we know, this is all now moot.

Snoops now has his own shelf in the 'bathroom', stuffed with myriad different conventional drugs (blood tests found he also has a failing liver, so he has to take orange Smartie-like tablets for that), and an apothecary of herbal remedies. I have to give him four small meals a day so that he can take all his medicine. If I feed him too much he throws up, like a cancer patient. He sometimes gets a runny tummy from all the medication, so I boil a few grains of Tilda rice to mix in with his food. He's still too weak to wash anything other than his face, and so I comb him gently every day, getting out the knots from his fur. I hate the way the comb knocks on his bones but when we are done he looks all smart and he still stretches his forehead towards me for his kiss. To get on my giant bed he uses a Matthew Hilton ottoman, which I had placed at the foot to help poor obese Squeaky, whose attempts to climb on board were frantic and doomed to failure – I would often see her face beside me momentarily on the pillow, wide-eyed, like an extreme mountaineer, before she would disappear from view with a thud. I'm sorry, Snoopy, I tell him as he tries to wobble up the stairs. I wonder who I'm keeping him alive for, me or him. It's at times like this that I miss my ex-husband.

CHAPTER 21

* * *

(In which my best friend tells me she is pregnant, and I feel churlish she has trumped my lambs)

My friend Kerry came down for the weekend. She was my PA at the glossy magazine and my deputy when I worked on the London *Evening Standard* for five long, latte-fuelled years. In all my years of journalism, I have only met half a dozen people whom I now count as friends and whose work I respect. Kerry is one of them.

On the glossy magazine, we would fly off to LA or New York to try to persuade stars to appear on the cover, or to attend cover shoots just to make sure the photographer – despite his £20,000-plus fee for lounging around all day eating the free buffet and listening to music and calling his friends and then, after all his assistants have done the work, pushing a shutter – doesn't go all mad and creative and shoot the star in black and white, or with their eyes shut, or just take a picture of their feet. This was a more common occurrence than you might imagine.

On the newspaper, if ever I went on holiday, Kerry would quake with nerves as this would be the time the editors higher up the pecking order would interfere and tell her off. Once, she snuck off to a yoga class in her lunch break, only to have the executive features editor phone the gym and persuade some poor feckless girl to brave the sweaty studio and haul Kerry's arse out of there, back to her desk. Sadly, gone are the days when journalists went out into the world to get their ideas. Ours were gleaned first from other newspapers and then, more recently, from the internet. Through all the stresses and strains of setting up features for the magazine and then the newspaper, Kerry proved herself a good sort. She never lost her sense of humour. At the end of a 12-hour day, waiting for proofs of our pages to be passed by the editor, we would order a takeaway, crack open a bottle of wine, put our high heeled-clad feet up on the desk and dissect the men in our lives.

Kerry, as my PA, was in at the birth, as it were, of my relationship with my future husband; she could conceivably have been in at the actual birth of my future husband, so young was he when we met. He'd come to my office to interview me for his local radio news slot (my magazine was up for an award; we didn't win, and I felt as I had when I returned to find my equestrian wooden spoon had not warranted a prize) and had, rather cheekily, phoned the office the next day to ask for my email address. Kerry would only give him hers and so his invitation to meet for coffee met her saucer-shaped eyes first. She liked him, so she encouraged me.

It was sad but, amongst all the women on the magazine, I was the only one who was still single and so I felt under a great deal of pressure to catch up. Looking at these floaty top-clad young women each morning as they arrived for work, it was easy to see why they had romantic success and I didn't. They were invariably late, they were dressed sexily and über-casually, they then chatted on their mobiles for what seemed like hours, and then they logged onto their computers, browsing property websites to find somewhere appropriate in which to nest. They all found poor antiquated me, someone who hardly had time to say hello to them, who always had my coffee and Marmite on toast brought to my desk, who always wore a sharp Helmut Lang trouser suit, who worked late, who never even attempted to do yoga at lunchtime, unenviably driven and super-busy. They certainly didn't aspire to be like me, oh Jesus Christ no. They shrank with fear as I swept past their desks, and tapped ever more feverishly on their computer keyboards for places to go on holiday, tips on how to get pregnant, country piles where they could quickly organise a wedding reception.

Kerry was the only one who was remotely like me, a mini me in fact. When she arrived for the weekend with her husband in tow (yes, she'd got married, but I had thought like me she'd just leave him at home and ignore him, like an expensive new gadget she didn't have time to read the instructions for), I could see from the moment she stepped out of their borrowed, gleaming new 4x4 that she was pregnant. 'Oh my God!' I screamed as I hugged her. She looked tired and bashful but happy. Her husband, a great big bear of a man, exactly like Aidan in *Sex and the City*, was so attentive, so proud of her, it was sweet to watch. I'd been looking forward to her coming down for girly chats and endless chewing over people we know from work, but all she wanted to do was talk about the baby and go to bed early. I felt a bit deflated, actually. I had all these things to show her, the horses and the dog slash boyfriend, the chickens, the extraordinary colour of the trees as their leaves turn crisp and orange and bright yellow and flame red, but nothing really measures up to a human baby. Well, it does to me, of course, but to a newly married couple in love expecting a human baby, any sort of animal menagerie doesn't amount to a hill of beans.

On the Saturday night, me and Kerry sat in front of the apple log fire, talking. Her husband had gone to bed. I asked her why she thought things hadn't turned out right for me in my marriage (you perhaps can understand now why I no longer have many friends). 'I think he was sweet when you met him, but then he changed. You were too nice to him. The success, your success, the bits that rubbed off onto him, went straight to his head. You need someone older, someone generous, someone who will buy you things for a change.'

'But I don't want someone to buy me things, to look after me.'

'But Kevin looks after me. It doesn't make me weak, or anything less than who I am. It's nice. It makes him feel good too.'

I suppose I've never been one of those women who are comfortable being taken on holiday or bought dinner because I've never valued my own company that much. God, a man, any man, would want his money back after a holiday spent with me. I wouldn't want him to see me in a bikini, or have sex with the lights on, or without my face on. I hate the lighting on planes, especially in the loo. I looked up at my reflection in a plane loo once and saw Thora Hird staring back at me.

I threw a couple more logs on the fire, despite the fact poor pregnant Kerry was yawning. 'I came to live in a wilderness partly because I knew no one would see me if I couldn't be arsed to get dressed properly or put make-up on,' I told Kerry sadly. 'I don't want anyone to watch me become old.'

'But my God, Lizzie, you're lovely,' she said, hugging me and making Michael jealous, so he squeezed between us. 'And neurotic, and plagued by OCD – although, I have to say, you seem slightly better here. I had expected the wellies to be all lined up, freshly hosed.'

I realise now why I chose my husband. Oh, okay, he pursued me, a little bit, what 26-year-old male wouldn't chase a mature woman with a good job, a car, house and nice clothes and quite a few handbags and who was, as he admitted if he ever caught sight of me by accident in the shower, in 'good nick'; how was he to know I didn't have any experience of being in a relationship beyond staring at a David Cassidy poster, that I was as novice and as hopeless at the whole thing as he was?

My being here in the countryside is just an adult version of reading pony books rather than having my nose stuck in *Fab 208*. I spent the weekends during my A levels mucking out and sitting in a freezing caravan eating peanut butter sandwiches – an avoidance tactic for real life. What I'm doing now is not real life. It's an escape. A pretty damn hard one, a bit like one of those Californian extreme boot camps where you keep going hiking on an empty stomach, but one in which I have opted out of the race, sort of gracefully. I'm happy for Kerry, think she will make a fantastic, patient mother, but I'm not jealous of what she has. The thought of getting up every day and putting another human being first would make me want to eat my own head. The older women I have met whom I have admired most have never been ones with children, who have sat in perfect Kensington morning rooms or suburban lounges surrounded by hundreds of pictures of their brood in various stages of development, who inhabit a warm cocoon where only the family and the children matter. The women I've admired most have been child-free. They seem more vital, more concerned about the great big world, more generous, far more interesting, far more interested. And the women I admire always, always, always are surrounded by animals they love. I think the most accurate way to measure a person's character is by how large and varied their wild birdfeeders are and how well stocked.

They left early the next morning. I felt tearful, as if I was never going to see her again. Kerry squeezed my hand and promised to come back with the baby next time, but I knew she would no longer have as much time for me, that things would never be the same between us again.

CHAPTER 22

* * *

(In which I get two dates in a month)

This is odd, pretty much unprecedented. This is almost 'double parking', my ex-friend Michelle's (yes, another one. I think she took offence when I wrote that her stomach measured four feet in circumference; in my defence, she was pregnant with twins at the time) term for when you have sex with two different men during the course of one weekend (not during the course of one night; that would be Daphne- or K*****-worthy whorishness), an event that has happened to me only once, in a halcyon period forever after known as 'my heyday'.

A couple of days after Kerry's visit, I have to go to London for work. I'm sitting in Home House, a club on Portland Square, sipping coffee, looking out the beautiful Georgian windows at a garden square and thinking, Oh God, I miss my old life. A blonde woman sits down next to me. I offer her my newspaper and we start talking. She's very warm and very Irish. She asks me what I'm doing in London, and I tell her a little bit about Exmoor, about the horses.

Whenever I tell anyone where I live they get all misty-eyed and I start to think, maybe it's me who has it all wrong. Maybe it's me who can never appreciate what I have.

'So, why on earth did you move there?' she asks me.

'I got divorced, needed a change, the usual.'

'Are you with anyone now?'

'Lord, no. I don't want to be with someone. Men are too much hard work, it's all so exhausting, grooming and honing yourself and having to listen to them tell you things and monitor their text messages and, besides, I don't have the time.'

'That's how I know you'll meet someone,' she says reassuringly. 'Because you're not desperate. You have your own life. You just might want to meet someone some day so you can have some fun.' I had forgotten about fun.

She carries on reading. I carry on fiddling with my BlackBerry. Every time I look at it, I think of brambles.

'I know a really nice man you ought to meet,' she says. 'Look at you! You're slim, attractive, got great hobbies. He's a millionaire. I won't tell him how old you are but let me set you up with him.'

'Oh no, please no. He won't like me. I live in the middle of nowhere in a crumbling ruin. I am a crumbling ruin.'

She tells me this mystery man lives in the country too, in Essex, and has an apartment in London. That would be useful, a very small part of me thinks, fleetingly. At least it would be somewhere I could thaw my feet. He's in wealth management, whatever that is. I reluctantly agree that she can give him my mobile number. The next day, I'm walking 'my new boyfriend' down the lane, he keeps disappearing into the hedges to sniff things, and I'm standing at the gate watching Lizzie in the square field. She's looking so well: fit, muscled, with hard, perfect feet and a relaxed expression. Standing there I'm sure I look like a mum on the school run – worn, tired, dirty, unmade-up, defeated – waiting for my beautiful child to emerge. I realise my life has become all about her, nothing about me. My phone burbles. Lizzie lifts her aristocratic head, irritated. I say hello. It's him – the Millionaire.

'Is that Liz?'

'Yes.'

'Hi. My friend Mairead said I should give you a call.'

'Oh God, what did she say about me?'

'She said you were gorgeous and mad about animals.'

'The second part is true.'

'I have a Labrador,' he says, and I start to warm to him. He sounds young, interested in me, normal. Not insane, anyway. There are no awkward silences, something I had become rather used to. He tells me what he likes to do in his spare time: take long walks, sit by log fires, stay in five-star hotels, eat in good restaurants. He sounds too good to be true.

'Is Mairead always setting you up with women?' I ask him, suddenly shy, suddenly back at a mid-Seventies Essex disco, trying to hear a conversation over the strains of 'Midnight at the Oasis'. I once won a beauty competition at the Zero 6 disco just outside Southend Airport; despite this, I didn't get one single date with a boy during a decade that was, for lots of people, all about free love, drugs, music festivals and Marvin Gaye ballads.

'No, no. She wouldn't dare. She knows how fussy I am.'

What is surprising about this phone call is that talking to him doesn't seem to suck the life blood, all the energy, from me. I don't have to try too hard. I don't have to keep saying, 'Are you all right? Are you sure? What's wrong? Can I buy you a car? Take you somewhere exotic on holiday, buy you a business-class ticket to India so you can get your end away?' For the first time in my life, I realise when I snap my phone off, I have actually been flirting.

We arranged to meet in a couple of days' time. He suggested the bar at the Connaught. I liked the fact he hadn't chosen a sandwich bar for vaguely proletarian, deeply flawed reasons (whenever I went somewhere nice with my husband, he made me feel guilty, as if sitting in a lovely art-deco bar was somehow oppressing someone in a Third World country. In the end, it all became a bit wearing). I find myself in a bit of a panic, wondering how on earth I can possibly get myself vaguely shipshape in such a short space of time.

Two days later, slightly breathless, I'm sat in the bar, the very dark bar, of the Connaught, sipping champagne, waiting for the Millionaire to turn up. Nic is staying over to look after the animals and sends me a picture of Squeaky sitting on her lap, dribbling on her arm. Sitting in this lovely bar, with my high heels on, my new season black lace Prada skirt that I bought with the last of my credit, suddenly no longer feels like me. While in the country,

I long for London, now, sat here, I long for the sight and smells of the moor, the silence, the mist trapped in pockets (not literally in my pockets, I mean in the dips of the valleys, but I suppose sometimes it does get trapped in my pockets), the feel of my lambs' soft, downy mouths on mine, the sound Lizzie makes when she blows through her nose. I look at the faces of the people around me, all of whom probably have warm, normal lives with families, and I no longer envy them.

This is stupid, I think. What am I even doing here? I'm about to get up and go when he arrives. He has brown, kind eyes (I'd always thought brown eyes were kind until I met my husband; no, that's mean, he is kind, just not kind to me) that twinkle. He's wearing a suit, which I remember as brown but which he'll later swear wasn't. I stand up, towering over him in my ridiculous platform shoes even though he's quite a normal height, not dwarfish like that other one, and he kisses me lightly on both cheeks. He has brought the cold, metallic London air with him. He doesn't knock anything over. He doesn't do a grizzly face, his mouth a Charlie Brown wiggly line, because we are somewhere vaguely posh. We sit down. I cross my legs and he glances at them. He orders me another glass of champagne (I've hidden the empty flute of my first one under my chair). We talk for a bit about Gordon Brown, the economy, animals: his and mine. I tell him that I've been married before, I don't know whether Mairead has mentioned it, and he tells me he'd read about it somewhere. Oh dear.

He tells me he has two grown-up sons, one at university,

the other something of a playboy (there would've been a time when I would've pursued the sons; you see, I am progressing, maturing). He talks quite a lot about his ex-wife, about how she was 'great eye candy' (aren't they always? My husband's concubines were always beautiful, breathtaking, clever, bendy, etc, etc, but I've seen their pictures on Facebook and I know they were ordinary, not great at punctuation or spelling, and with no self-awareness or sense of humour at all) but also boring and avaricious. She spent £500,000 of his money on divorcing him; he doesn't tell me why they split up in the first place, and I don't ask. She never lets him have the boys for Christmas. 'Surely they're old enough for it to be their choice?' I say. 'I suppose.' He says he used to drive a Ferrari, but now he's more sensible and drives a Bentley. I roll my eyes. I think he has a driver. I feel as if I'm Carrie, dating Mr Big.

I'm starting to think he might quite like me when he suddenly looks straight at me, asking a direct question I don't begin to understand, and when I try to mumble a reply and join in, he focuses on my face and says, 'Oh, I wasn't talking to you. I'm on Bluetooth.' Ye godfathers. I'd imagined we would talk late into the night, maybe go on somewhere for dinner, but after exactly one hour he sneaks a glance at his expensive watch, leans way back on his bar stool and asks for the bill. I stand up and start walking towards the rotating door without waiting for him, desperate to get in my car and motor west, take off my stupid shoes, step out of my skirt and pull on something daubed in mud. He hurries after me, and leaps round me to open my car door. There was a time, not so long ago, when I would've been mortified that when he opened my car door a bale of hay fell out, but now I don't give a monkey's; there's actually a potato sprouting in my glove compartment. Before the date I'd imagined him walking me to my car, slamming me against the boot, running a hand up my thigh, ruching my black lace Prada skirt and reaching up to my grey cashmere Prada knickers, pushing them aside with his hungry hands, kissing me roughly, suggesting we get a room. Oh, if only life was how we imagined it. If only this were indeed fiction.

Weirdly, the very next day, I get an email from my ex-husband. Maybe ex-husbands have a sixth sense, they can tell when you might be moving on, having fun, becoming interested in someone else, no matter that the someone else couldn't wait, it seemed, to get shot of me. 'Hey Liz, if you are ever in London, would you like to meet for coffee? Only if you have time and if you want to, that is.'

I stare at the message for a bit, trying to decipher what exactly it means. Is he still in love with me? Is he going to tell me face to face that he's got married to a 32-year-old Indian woman who wears brown lipliner and is already the mother of his unborn child? Is he going to tell me off? What?

As nonchalantly as I can, I type, 'Am in London on Sunday, do you want to have supper?'

'That would be lovely. As long as you don't spend too much.'

Well, that was almost a good response, so I book a table

at Locanda Locatelli on Seymour Street: a chic, quiet, dark Italian place. I wasn't going to be in London on a Sunday, of course, but there's something about communicating with my ex-husband that gags me from telling the truth. I suddenly become a different person, all nice and easy-going and accommodating when I should've just told him to bugger off. But I know that Sunday is also his birthday, his 35th, and so by asking if he is free for supper I'm not just being kind and spontaneous, it's a subtle way of finding out whether or not he's still single. Just out of curiosity. My desire for detail always gets me into trouble. Why are women like this? Why do we always want to know more? While I've just logged onto Daphne's Facebook page and found out she's given birth to a ginger baby, I bet the thought of checking up to see if she's happy or with someone or married hasn't even occurred to him. With men, it seems, once something moves away from directly under their nose, it's as if it doesn't exist. Perhaps, for men, the theory that the universe disappears as soon as we walk out the room is actually true.

And so, on Sunday morning, I rather rush Lizzie with her ablutions, which she doesn't take kindly to at all. I try to piece together my shattered, neglected body as best I can. I again pull into service the Prada black lace skirt and a plain white T-shirt, and dangle my silver sandals in my hand. I look at myself sideways in the mirror and I say to myself, hmm, you've still got it. Maybe all those expensive unguents weren't worth the money, after all; maybe what works best is fresh air, home-grown food and exercise.

I leave Michael with Nicola, yet again, and he gives me such a mournful, betrayed, cuckolded, beady brown stare I almost change my mind and don't go. I drive the four hours to London, quite excited to be doing something normal at last, something that doesn't involve field paste or pulling turnips (I don't even like turnips: horrid, round, hard things). Eventually, I park right outside the restaurant. I unfold myself from my low car like a deckchair and stagger to the door. I realise walking in heels takes practice, and I have somehow lost the knack. My feet must have spread, too, wearing wellies all the time, as the straps on my sandals are pinching.

London doesn't seem too bad on a Sunday when it's quiet and you have somewhere special to go. I suddenly feel all nostalgic for Selfridges. I sit in a brown leather booth, eating breadsticks and sipping champagne, which goes straight to my head. He arrives about 15 minutes late, something of a record. He looks impossibly young and handsome, but he's wearing a green shiny anorak, and underneath is the brown striped acrylic sweater I've always hated. He leans across the table to kiss my cheek and knocks over the bottle of Pellegrino water. I ignore the encroaching fizzy puddle. 'I cut my hair,' I tell him, swinging it glossily around my neck. I had grown tired of it turning into a bird's nest given the howling wind on Exmoor, and had done what all women do when they pass 50: got a choppy bob. I had started to regret losing my mane, my 'horse hair', as my husband used to call it but, after all, there is no one to see it any more, and anyway I am, nowadays, invariably wearing a hard hat, a hoodie or a Burberry Beanie. 'It looks lovely,' he says, surprised. 'Makes you look younger.' God, don't I hate it when people say that? As if all we want is to look younger. I know 19-year-olds who don't look as good as I do. He doesn't ask if I'm dating anyone, but apropos of nothing I tell him that I am. He doesn't ask a single question about my mythical new inamorato, merely looks surprised, and continues chewing, like a sheep.

We talk about his trip to India. He'd gone there travelling for a while and wasn't sure he'd be going back. He's living in Ealing with his mum again. 'How's that working out?' I ask him, thinking, 'You once had a Georgian house, your own office and high-definition TV.' He tells me she got on his nerves that morning, saying that if he continues to walk around the house without socks on, he'll catch a cold. 'I had to tell her to shut up, shut up!' he says, doing an impression of himself cross. I remember that voice, that expression, those words, and am so glad he no longer tells me the same thing. He's going to wait and see if things 'take off' for him in London. I feel sad, seeing him like this, and I wonder if he's sad, too. Is he really glad to be shot of me or does he want it back the way it was, maybe without the infidelity part and the being hit with a trainer part. He orders fish and we have a slight argument about this. I tell him that some fish, coi, for example, live to be 40 years old, so how can you possibly eat them? He tells me that in India he met the most boring, self-important vegan Buddhists and the nicest, most generous, warm, meat-eating Muslims, so I shouldn't be so dictatorial. I'm outraged. I tell him I don't care whether someone being a vegan makes them a good host, a nice person, well-read, interesting or even (this last part the most important where he is concerned) a good shag; I care whether an animal is alive or not. Whether an animal has suffered. I remember how infuriating and intractable he can be.

After dinner, we get up to leave, he puts his anorak back on and asks if I would be going out of my way if I dropped him at his mum's. I'm not relishing the four-hour drive back to Exmoor, and so I say yes, I can drop him off. No problemo. We drive in almost silence, which I soon realise is due to the fact he's fallen asleep. He later tells me he had been out very late the night before, at a club in King's Cross, celebrating his birthday. Sometimes you need small reminders of what you had but don't miss. I drop him off, he pecks me goodbye like that tortoise again, saying he's glad to see me looking so happy, and I speed away. It has been almost nine years since I first dropped him outside his mum's after our very first date. A few months ago, I would've wished that I could have gone back to that night and changed everything, done everything differently. Now, though, I'm not quite so sure.

CHAPTER 23

* * *

(In which I lose the best friend I will ever have. The love of my life)

Snoopy is dead. The day before yesterday, he was fine: eating well, sunbathing, taking his tablets. I'd combed his fur so he looked all smart. But yesterday morning I woke up, and immediately called for Snoopy. He was in his cupboard, on my Liberty white towel. He said hello, and I told him I'd get his breakfast. I came back with his M&S tuna, with the first of his many tablets. He ate it lying down. I held his water bowl next to his head because he seemed unable to sit up. The only way he could move was by pulling himself along by his front paws. I fed him from my fingers. I noticed that his eyes, his bright, green, kind, wise eyes, were retreating into his head. I called the holistic vet, who was at a party. Oh, I thought, the days when I went to parties. He gave me lots of advice, and we concluded Snoops didn't seem to be in any pain. I considered calling out an emergency vet, but in my heart felt that all Snoopy really wanted was to be allowed to sleep on his special towel. I kept holding the bowl to his small mouth (he always looks as though he's smiling) so that he could drink.

I didn't leave his side. I watched episode after episode of *24*, trying to keep awake. At half past midnight I went into the bathroom to find Snoopy in his litter tray, fast asleep. He is such a dignified cat, he had crawled to his tray, but been unable to get out again. I lifted him gently (he weighed nothing), and placed him back on his towel.

This morning, I got up at six and could barely make myself go into the bathroom, so terrified was I of what I might find. But Snoopy said hello, and looked me right in the eye: a long, slow, steady stare. He hadn't moved an inch. I tried putting food next to his head, but he batted it away. I called my local vet. She said she would come as soon as she could. I lay on the floor, stroking Snoopy in his cupboard. He kept purring, and I kept telling him what a good friend he had been to me, always. I told him that in 17 years, he had never given me anything but love. That every time I left the house, I had counted the minutes until I saw him again. His breathing seemed to slow, and I called the vet. 'Where the f*** are you!!' I shouted. I dripped some water on his mouth, which he drank greedily. I told him how much I loved him. At about 11.30 in the morning he suddenly let out this great big howl, his tongue came out of his mouth, and he arched his back in my arms. I held his head. I looked into his eyes, and they were like glass. My tears plopped onto him, making his fur wet. I held his ears and his white paws as they grew cold. When the vet came, she listened for his heartbeat. 'He's gone,' she said. I asked her about a million times if she was sure. I told her my biggest fear was burying him alive. I wrapped him in two of my cashmere sweaters that still smelled of me, and placed him in a box with his favourite toy. He still had food on his nose that he'd been too weak to wash off. Brian (Brain) the gardener dug him a grave in the spot by the washing line, where Susie passes by each day. As I laid his box in the red earth, I turned to see Susie, Squeaky and Sweetie standing, watching, in a line like the Three Degrees. They knew exactly what was happening. I miss him so much already and it's only been a couple of hours. I don't think he wanted to leave me. He so loved being a cat. I so loved having him in my life.

CHAPTER 24

* * *

(In which I find myself in the middle of a hedge, looking for moths)

I'm standing in Emily's shop, sheltering from the rain. I tell her I figure I have to join in more, make more of a life down here. 'The woman in the gift shop two doors down, before you get to the gun shop and the toy shop, keeps suggesting she should decorate my Christmas tree, get in the groceries every Friday, warm the house up, get in logs, that sort of thing,' I tell her. 'What does she think I am, completely useless?'

Emily's hair is now in a long cascade of ringlets and some of it has been dyed blonde. She is so buxom and healthy-looking she looks like a character in *Lark Rise to Candleford*. 'The woman in the gift shop is called Linda,' she tells me sternly. 'I don't know how you still don't know her name.' I tell Emily that not so long ago I did a deal with a woman who has a farm about two miles from me. In return for occasionally being able to school her horse in my manège, she says I can ride across her land. The other day, out with 'my new boyfriend', I saw what I thought was her on a horse, only for it not to be her at all but another equestrian neighbour who now, because of my confusion and then my desperately trying to cover it up, uses my manège as well. Emily laughs. 'People think you only live here at weekends.' I make a shocked face and grasp her counter. 'They never see you at anything. You just don't seem to want to join in. I hear you swore at a woman in a 4x4 the other day because she didn't slow down sufficiently going past your horse.'

I remember I had sworn at the woman and actually shaken my fist at her retreating vehicle. People are so blasé about animals in this part of the world; how does she know that Lizzie isn't frightened of cars? What if one of my cats had been in the road, or Michael? Every day my heart breaks at the sight of dead animals on the side of the road: foxes, great big badgers, rabbits. 'I never have the time to get to know anyone. But then, neither do you, you're always working,' I say.

'But I've always lived here. I went to school here. I know everyone. I have a shop. People think you hide away on your farm, scowling at anyone with a gun or a spaniel.' I suppose she's right. The only occasion I've been out locally since moving down here is when I attended a talk on colic at Tiverton Rugby Club.

'But I don't agree with hunting. I don't understand the desire to live in the countryside if you don't love the wildlife. It doesn't make any sense to me. Why live here, where it's all peaceful, and make a noise shooting? Why not take joy from watching the rabbits playing rather than shoot them?'

She tells me that local life isn't all about killing things.

'There is a Tae Kwon Do club, there's a yoga class in the village hall every Wednesday evening ...'

'God, no. I think people who do yoga are dirty time-wasters. Meditation is just laziness.'

'You could decorate the church with flowers or join the WI and learn how to make jam. You could write a poem for the Dulverton newsletter.' She's teasing me now. She hands me two leaflets. One is for a 'moth morning', whatever in God's name that is. The second is news of an open audition for the Christmas play. She tucks both into the box of organic Cox's apples I have just bought for the horses.

'Jesus. I thought moths came out at night and banged around on light bulbs.'

It's 5 am and I have just come out of a hedge, backwards. I now know what people look like when they actually do this, and I have to say it isn't great. I'm on a beautiful stretch of common in a place called East Anstey, on the edge of the moor. The group of wrapped-up-warm people with me are either about six years old or six hundred years old; I'm the only person vaguely in the middle and who has a mouth without any great big gaps. These people are all members of the Somerset Moth Group, lepidopterists who don't just observe these shy little creatures but trap them as well. I would've thought this was against the law, what with the fuss about the bats and the newts. I don't agree with trapping anything, but perhaps they just tag the moths and then let them go.

I cannot understand the propensity in the country for

doing things so early in the day, but everyone else seems cheerful, interested and alert. We all have torches and we are standing by the hedge trying to spot rare moths. The purpose of our moth morning is to count them, identify rare breeds and to 'promote interest of these fascinating creatures'. Macro moths are the big ones, micro moths are the little ones. I never knew, or even imagined in my wildest dreams, there were so many species of moth. There are chestnut-coloured carpet moths, the Dwarf Cream, the Small Dusty Wave. The Hedge Rustic and the Northern Drab. A moth suddenly flutters past me and, as if by instinct, I start flapping my arms and screaming. I suddenly understand that the point of these mornings is not to frighten the moths or, worse, turn them into brown smudges on your arm by mistake (who knew that moths were so fragile?), but to love them and appreciate them. The most common moths we see are the Pale Brindled Beauty and the Oak Beauty. I wonder which one of the little buggers has been responsible for eating my sweaters.

That same evening, I'm in the local wine bar with Nic. We've become so merry on cider that a passing group of (old) men assumed we were on a hen night. I have forced Nic to come along with me to audition for the Moor the Merrier Players' Christmas production. 'I hate plays,' she says. 'You can't hate plays,' I tell her. 'Yes I can, it's all showing off.' I show her the leaflet. The production the amateur dramatic society has rather ambitiously decided to stage this year is *The Match Girls*. This seems a little bit of a gloomy choice for a musical to me, as it's all about the fact girls who worked in the match factories of Dickensian London had no rights and suffered from poisoning by phosphorus, a condition called 'phossy jaw'. Nic and I shuffle unsteadily to the town hall, which is freezing and has that awful smell you get in school sports halls (sort of feet mixed with damp and mashed potato). There are already ten or so people standing around chatting. 'Hello!' shouts a small man who looks as though he might once have been in the military. 'So good to see you!'

It turns out, bar a couple of nerdy, overweight children, that Nic and I are considered in this group to be 'the young entry' (Nic is 39; I, as you know full well, am no longer in my prime), which gives you some idea of the precise vintage of everyone else. There is a youngish man sat in a corner, but judging by the state of him (he reeks of alcohol and urine), I think he's just here to keep out of the rain. Everyone is quite sweet to him, offering him plastic cups of coffee and a plate of biscuits with jam in the middle. I can see he could probably be quite handsome if he was clean and had a more normal expression. I always feel sad when I see a homeless person or an alcoholic, imagining them when they were babies: all sweet, perfect and unspoilt.

The military man and his wife, who is blonde and wearing a huge necklace of plastic baubles, are obviously in charge. The woman once did something 'in the West End'. We all pull chairs into a circle, bar the young man, who has now peed on the floor. No one asks him to leave. We are each handed a script. As there are so few of us, it seems we all automatically get a part. Nic, who has quite a good voice, gets the part of Kate, the young heroine, a tenement girl and worker at the Bryant and May factory in the East End of London. I am to be Mrs P, an old crone, with just one song: 'Look at that hat'. (It dawns on me much, much later that the P refers to Pankhurst.) I'm to wear black, a grey bun and a bonnet, and have an old woman's face drawn by Betty who works in the pharmacy, on top of the one I already have. As we all get ready for a first read through, Nic hisses at me: 'I could be at home right now, watching Kiefer Sutherland in *24*. Anyway, I don't want to meet new people. I don't even have enough time for the friends I already have. I already have a perfectly nice boyfriend.'

'But it's for charity!' I wail unconvincingly (it's all in aid of some new lighting in All Saints Church), realising as I say this that there is no backing out now. I have committed myself to making a complete fool of myself because I can't sing or act. At least I suppose I'll be in a fairly heavy disguise. I have to add here that I did, once, improbably, get a B grade A level in Drama and Theatre Arts, despite a desultory performance as Olivia in *Twelfth Night*. I had only taken that A level because I fancied a fellow student called Chris. I was so besotted, I actually followed him up to London to share a flat with him (he got in to the Central School of Speech and Drama), paid for an audition at RADA, then failed to turn up as I was so upset that John Lennon had died that same morning. I then decided, heady with the success of Zero 6, that I wanted to be a model, so I went to see Laraine Ashton, who told me it wasn't because I was too short that she was turning me down, it was because my skin was so bad!

I then pretended that I did, in fact, want to work in fashion as an editor, after all, and got a job on my first magazine. Anyway, as you can see from this weird trajectory from failed thespian to fashion and magazine editor, it was all driven by a crush, and by failure. I never became an actress, I never became a model. I never, even, became Chris's girlfriend. I came home one day to find him in bed with a movie star.

At 10 pm, Nic and I go back to the wine bar to warm up by the log burner. She orders a latte, and tells them to replace the milk with Bailey's, and I ask to look at the wine list. I choose something white and dry (a bit like me, etc), and as it's so delicious ('Life is too short to drink cheap wine!' a notice on the wall chirrups happily), I ask if I can take a bottle home with me. I'm told I have to order it, and so am given a book to write down my name and phone number. And there, in the book, right above where I'm now scribbling my order, is the name and address of a very famous rock star. I notice he lives on the moor, quite near where I went to that awful New Year's Eve party. I now vaguely remember that I'd read in one of those 'where are they now' features that he gave up the drugs and the women, and disappeared to make cheese, or cider, or open a hotel, I can't quite recall which. I nudge Nic. 'Look,' I say, pointing to his name. 'He's proper crumpet,' she says. 'Probably a bit before my time but I remember seeing him on *Top of the Pops* in a pair of black Lycra leggings.'

I don't tell her that, back in the very early Eighties, I interviewed this rock star when I worked on my first women's magazine. He was between marriages at the time, and I had stupidly thought he might fancy me. Of course, he didn't. I think he was off his face on coke or heroin or some such, and halfway through the interview I could tell he was getting bored with my line of questioning. 'Anything else?' he'd asked. At the end of our designated 45 minutes, he shook my hand and said, as he showed me out of his hotel suite (I think it was at the Dorchester), 'Thank you for your support.' What a f***ing liberty, as Catherine Tate would say. I vowed, then and there, never to try to meet someone by setting up an interview with them (although it worked for my husband, though, didn't it? And that TV reporter with the big mouth who ended up with Al Pacino?). I no longer listen to his band's records; I have them all on cassette, but I don't think cassettes work any more, they're as obsolete as hobble skirts (oh God, I rue the day I ever agreed to play a bloody suffragette). We go out into the night and I drive home. Michael will be getting worried.

CHAPTER 25

* * *

(In which I acquire an agoraphobic bag of nerves: she is, it seems, just like her new mummy)

Every time I motor along the M5 I notice on my left, stood in a small scrub of land, a horse. She (or he, I'm usually going quite fast) never seems to be grazing, and despite the fact it might be snowing, or minus seven degrees, she or he is never wearing a rug. What worries me most is that the horse seems to be in the middle of a rubbish tip: there are old bedsteads, the skeletons of cars and lorries, and unlit bonfires. One morning, on my way to London at about 7 am, I see her and I almost slam on my brakes. She's on her knees, her head touching the frosty ground. I decide to leave at the next exit and see if I can find her. What I will do if I can locate her I have no idea; I only know that I cannot continue to look the other way.

I leave the motorway and circle left. I try to keep the M5 on my left, but it's hard. I drive around stupidly for about an hour until I come across a lane that seems to be pointing in the right direction. I take it, passing rusty, abandoned Land Rovers (farmers are so untidy), and come to a broken metal gate. I get out of the car, inappropriate in my heels and skirt, and tiptoe towards the gate (it's padlocked) to peer over. And there's the horse. I can see she's a mare, and she is up now, but still with her head hanging low. I climb over the gate. I cannot see any water and the ground is worse than I had imagined: very rutted, and no grass at all. I walk up to her, making the noises horses expect, and I can see she's in a terrible state. She's very dark brown, almost black, with a short, pulled mane, no forelock to speak of, a great big thick tail and a tiny white star in the middle of her forehead. I don't know how old she is because I haven't learned how to read teeth. She has shoes on. She is obviously a thoroughbred, about 16 hands 2 inches: bigger than Lizzie, thicker set and not as fine. But lovely. She barely raises her eyes. I touch her neck: it's concave. I can feel every bone in her spine, and her hip bones are like the spokes on a broken umbrella. She is wearing a headcollar that is far too small for her: it's beginning to eat into her flesh. She has an old wound on her chest. 'Oooh, little lady,' I say. 'You are in a bad way.' I'm angry with myself for not having taken this detour months before. I can't see a shelter, or a nearby house. Reluctantly, I leave her. I teeter to my car, and tear a piece of paper from my Filofax. I write a note: 'Could the owner of this horse please telephone me on xxxxx; I would very much like to buy her.' I prop it between the gate and the post. I hope it doesn't blow away. I've found people always respond to offers of money. Reluctantly, I drive away; her eyes follow me and I think of the small brown mare I left behind in

Ethiopia, and the sound she made when she was calling for her foal.

About a week later, I get a phone call. It's from a woman and she says she's the owner of the horse. I don't immediately go on the attack, but instead ask her for the mare's story. 'Her stable name is Maggie. She had been competed as an eventer, but became dangerous at competitions,' she says. 'She would rear and run backwards. She couldn't take the pressure. Then it got that we couldn't get past cows: she would bolt across a main road if she saw one. I kept a cardboard cut-out of a cow in the stable next to her, but that didn't work. To be honest, I couldn't afford to keep her at livery if she wasn't up to doing competitions. She has caused rows between me and my boyfriend.'

It turns out things got so heated that her boyfriend stabbed the mare in the chest, so the woman moved her to this 'field' to be out the way and enjoy a short 'holiday'. I find it unbelievable that she would've allowed her boyfriend to have harmed her horse: she is like one of those awful mothers who don't put their children before their new boyfriends. Not only does the horse have no shelter, no rugs, no extra feed, no water, she is completely alone. You should never keep a horse on its own, but day after day I pass them, solitary, bored, not allowed to be in a herd, with no other horse to nibble their necks, to guard them while they sleep on the ground, to love them. 'Surely there are charities that would've taken her in?' I ask the woman. 'The RSPCA have been down to have a look at her — some idiot phoned them, saying she looked thin – so I did start feeding her again. I do love her, you know.'

Isn't it easy to say you love someone or something? I stupidly, rashly, offer the wretched woman two grand for the horse. I don't care about getting the horse vetted, or trying her out first to see if she can be ridden. I just have to get her out of the rubbish tip. The woman snaps it up; she says the money will enable her to buy 'a youngster, a three-year-old I can start myself'. I raise my eyes heavenwards and arrange to pick the horse up the following Sunday.

Well, she is here. I met the woman at the field and, to her credit, she was standing there with about six rugs in a pile on the ground, and a big bag of feed. The woman had taken the headcollar off and I could see the dents in Maggie's face where it had cut into her. I slipped Lizzie's headcollar on her, the one with the sheepskin noseband and brow band, which makes it nice and soft. Her face is beautiful, with slightly protruding, intelligent eyes that look about her, nervously, thinking, 'Oh blimey, what on earth will I be asked to do next?' She blew on my face. I snapped on the lead rope and walked her up the ramp of the horsebox, hired for the day with a driver who told me that, what with the current recession, he is taking 'three or four horses a week, good horses, young ones, nothing at all wrong with them' to the abattoir. People can no longer afford to keep them, he said, but I wonder whether they keep their cars, and their private educations, and their organic food, and their Nintendo Wiis. When we got Maggie to the farm, Nic was waiting anxiously by the gate. She was quite keen to get her hands on this little mare. 'Dangerous!' she shouted when I had slowly led Mags into her box and told her what had happened. She ran her fingers over the mare's back, down her legs, and lifted up her hooves, one by one, to peer at the soles. She has a very small left or near foot, with a frog that has been compacted by ill-fitting shoes, harbouring infection. Her feet actually smell, as though they are rotting. 'She is in a great deal of pain,' said Nic as she started to go through the rugs, examining the ingredients on the bag of feed. 'She has bruising on her withers, a misplaced pelvis, a very sore back. There is no way in hell I would even considering putting a saddle on her at the moment, let alone riding her cross-country.'

We watch the new horse in her stable. She sniffs the straw, paws it, and stales (horsespeak for has a wee). She does a twirl, and then settles down to eat her hay. I put a lightweight duvet rug on her; anything heavier would've made her wince. I tell Nic what the field was like. In a few moments, the mare rolls, covering her mane and tail in straw. She then lies down, exhausted. Her chin is resting on the rubber matting. She closes her great big eyes and then opens them wide in a flash. It's as if she has just gone to bed and then thinks, 'Oh bugger, I forgot to lock the front door.'

The next morning, I decide to turn her out to graze with the others. Lizzie is positively bursting to meet her. She is leaning over the gate onto the yard, whinnying, showing the bright red of her nostrils. I put on a turnout rug – again, one that is not too heavy – and I clip-clop her to the field. It's so strange, hearing the sound of a horse with shoes again. I lead her into the field and immediately she throws herself on the ground to roll, manically. She does this again and again. This is classic displacement activity: she is trying to deal with over-whelming stress. I slip off her headcollar (you should never leave them alone with a headcollar on; it could become caught in something) and she whirls round and then, like a bullet, gallops flat out to the other end of the field. I don't think I've ever seen a horse shift so fast, not even at the Grand National. I trot slowly after her. She is standing, shaking, in a far corner. From the skid marks you can tell she only just about managed to stop, narrowly avoiding plunging into the thick hedge. I put her head-collar on again and try to move her away from the hedge, but she refuses to budge. I assume she has just frightened herself.

I return a couple of hours later and she's still in exactly the same spot. I lead her to the middle of the field, but she boings back to her corner. There's a deep muddy patch on the ground where she has been rolling and rolling. I go back to check her again. It's now nearly dark. She's still in the corner. She's very tucked up, which means her stomach has contracted as she has not eaten or drunk anything; if horses don't eat all the time they can get colic and die. I put her headcollar on and lead her back to the yard and into her stable, where she immediately takes a long, cool drink, her eyes blinking at me as she drinks. I call Nic. She reckons the horse is agoraphobic, and starts madly Googling to find out how on earth we're going to treat her.

So, I now have a horse who's afraid to be in a field. I call the woman who owned her. 'I told you that,' she shouts. 'That's why I had her on such small pasture.' Stupid cow. When I get her passport, I find out she is 12 years old. From the vet's notes, I see she has splints on her legs (these are a sign a horse was worked too young or too hard). For now, I decide to just allow her to be a horse for a bit. I put her in the orchard with the lambs, who get quite excited at having someone new to follow around. I know it's going to take huge time, effort and patience to sort her out. I wonder what could have happened to her to make her fly into such a panic? I wonder what on earth made her afraid of the great outdoors? Lizzie keeps looking at me with a smug expression, as if to say, 'Hmm, so now who's the naughty one?'

CHAPTER 26

* * *

*(In which my shining hour arrives, and I'm
wearing old lady make-up and a grey wig)*

On Christmas Eve morning, my BlackBerry sprang
merrily into life. It was a text from the Millionaire.
'Merry Christmas, hope you're having a wonderful day.
I have to say I found you great company, funny and, dare
I say it, sexy! Love x' Although this was the only contact
from the outside world I received over the holiday period,
apart from a text from Orange, I was buoyed by the fact
he had got in touch at such a festive time of year. I re-
read the message, trying to decipher it. Then I started to
think that, maybe, it had been a round robin to all the
people in his address book. I didn't hold out much hope
for this one, to be honest. If he'd really fancied me, if
I were indeed going to be the Angelina Jolie to his Brad
Pitt, he would have called me by now, just to flirt a little.
I realised I was going to be spending New Year's Eve on
my own, yet again, unless of course you count the animals,
in which case it was all going to be a bit crowded.

I sat there, reading his text over and over again, trying
to decipher its hidden meaning, if any, his precise level of

keenness, what the 'x' might signify. I looked at the message again and thought, hmm, he used the word 'love'. And then I thought, why am I obsessing over a missive from a man I hadn't even fancied that much? Why am I even interested in someone who likes fancy restaurants and drives a Bentley? Why have I not learned that men might type an 'x', or even an 'X', but that doesn't mean they want to kiss you? I used to read all sorts of things into my husband's emails and texts, trying to gauge his level of affection for me. Several times I didn't end our marriage and gave him another chance because he'd happened to add two 'x's instead of the usual one, or referred to me as 'sweetheart'. Only later, when I hacked into his messages to other people, even complete strangers, and male ones at that, did I realise he failed to retain any special epithet for poor old me.

I'm in the local pub, feeling a little let down. I'm surrounded by bits of tinsel and the sound of people having a good time. I've just delivered my second performance of Christmas Eve as Mrs P. Neither went particularly well. In the matinee performance, to about two dozen people, including the young man who wees, my long black skirt had become caught under a wooden street barrow and so I'd had to deliver my song, 'Look at that hat', totally motionless (I hadn't really sung it; I'd spoken it in an extreme Cockney accent, a bit like Dick Van Dyke, although an unhelpful person pointed out to me in the tea and coffee with biscuits break that, in fact, Mrs Pankhurst had been quite posh, or at least middle class. Why had no one pointed this out earlier?). In the evening performance, the lead actor who played the part of the factory owner had come down with vomiting and diarrhoea (he had probably eaten one too many mouse-droppings-covered rum babas), and so the stand-in had had to go on in his place. He hadn't bothered learning the script, and so just walked around reading his words from the page. For some reason, this and the fact he had leaned on the 'flats' (the makeshift walls of the factory that had been painted to look like bricks by local schoolchildren) and made them wobble made me almost spontaneously combust with laughter. Nic kept shooting me devilish looks. She'd quite got into her singing and was giving it all she'd got. I couldn't wait to escape after it had all finished, and after taking off my black gown I pulled on my jodhpurs and boots, and my matted pink sweater, and didn't even bother washing off the hideous make-up. The grey bun was by now hanging over one ear. As, over the past 12 months, I've grown not to care what I look like, I didn't give my odd appearance a second thought.

Nic's boyfriend, Kevin, who looks so well established at a corner table I have a sneaky feeling he might have snuck out of the performance during the interval, goes up to the bar to get us each a drink. There's an ancient green man's hunting jacket hanging by the fireplace, and I tell Nic I'm going to ask if I can buy it. 'Why would you want to wear a jacket that was worn while chasing and killing things?' she asks me loudly. 'I want to look stylish and nice on Lizzie. Everyone, everything, deserves a second chance.' She raises her eyebrows. At the next table, Emily raises a glass to us. She nods towards the bar. I see someone with slim hips leaning over talking to the owner. He has grey, curly hair to his collar. Emily's eyes widen, then she looks away and starts talking pointedly to her boyfriend. Kevin returns, cradling three glasses, and carefully puts them down in front of us. 'Do you know who that is?' he says, indicating with his head the man in the jeans. 'No,' says Nic. He says his name. It's the rock star. 'Oh my goodness!' I say, craning my neck to look at him. 'I was totally, completely in love with him once.'

'Did you ever meet him?' asks Nic, doing an impression of a telescope, a bit like Squeaky when she is sitting on the sofa, waiting for me to come and join her, wondering where I am.

'Yes, I did actually. In the early Eighties. He was a bit of an arrogant prick, to be honest.' Because I'm quite deaf, I tend to talk quite loudly without noticing I'm doing so. At the word prick, he turns towards us. I can now see his round, rather piggy blue eyes. He stares at me. I think I blush. I remember one of the times I'd been to see him at Wembley. He had shaken his head and a drop of his sweat had landed on my face. I had dipped my finger in it and tasted it. It was probably the most erotic moment of my entire life. I think, wow, he must remember me. But then I realise I'm wearing old lady make-up, with deep, grey grooves painted each side of my nose, and crow's feet etched at the side of my eyes. My eyebrows have been obliterated, and a large mole has been appliquéd on the end of my nose. I put a hand to my face in a desperate attempt to cover it up and feel something furry creeping over one ear. My grey bun. I quickly tear it from my head. By now he must be thinking that I'm experiencing the after-effects of an extreme bout of chemotherapy. I gaze sadly into my glass and tell Nic to shovel herself along a bit to block me from his view. 'What am I, a pile of horse manure? What is wrong with you?'

The owner comes to our table. The rock star has twisted round and now has his elbow on the bar, listening. 'Did you enjoy that bottle of wine?' he asks me, wiping our table. Now I must seem like an alcoholic. All the drinking must have prematurely aged me. 'Um, yes, delicious.'

'We enjoyed your performance.' He and the rock star start laughing.

I do now actually crash my head onto the table, making all the glasses jump. The rock star comes over. No one else is taking any notice of him. I remember the rock star went into rehab in the early Nineties. Maybe he's coming over to counsel me, to offer to be my sponsor. He pulls out a chair, sits backwards on it, riding it like a horse. Sometimes, when I'm stressed, I lose my head. 'I didn't think men sat like that any more,' I say, thinking I'm safe behind my ancient disguise. 'Liz Jones,' he says simply.

Nic is quite impressed he knows my name. It turns out he's read some of my articles, and a couple of years ago had sent me an email when I had written that I had, at long last, after several decades of unrequited lust, got over my crush on him. 'I hear you've gone off me,' he had written. 'But I didn't think that was you,' I say now. 'Just some nutter with the same name.'

Nic pointedly starts talking to her boyfriend. 'I don't usually look this bad,' I say, rubbing at the Max Factor panstick. His grey hair is disconcerting. His eyes look different, no longer framed in kohl. He's very thin. Maybe he has to forage on Exmoor as well. He tells me he has a lurcher, two pigs, chickens and a small dairy herd. He doesn't mention a wife. After I'd read about his third marriage, I'd lost interest in him a bit, having my hands full with real boyfriends ('full' is a bit of an overstatement, I admit, for my sorry dating history. All that hope, all that expectation, and I spent as long in nappies as my two years' worth as a sexual being) for a change rather than imaginary ones. 'No horses?'

'No, I always fancied getting on board one though, feeling all that power between my legs,' he says saucily, and he has a twinkle in his eye. A man comes over to him and he stands up, whipping the chair from between his legs. 'Nice seeing you,' he says. I hide the grey bun under a soggy beer mat.

CHAPTER 27

* * *

*(In which I shuffle around like Mrs Overall,
and realise my animals look after me,
not the other way around)*

I can't stop thinking about him. I'm tempted to try to find my cassettes of his albums. Oh, that I wasn't a minimalist and hadn't thrown out my old, giant ghetto blaster. I think the reason I'm reading so much into this chance encounter with another living, breathing human being is that, with the new year looming ominously in front of me, I'm starting to panic that John the postman will one day find me frozen solid having fallen head-first into a water trough. Temperatures on Exmoor have plummeted to minus seven degrees, which means at all times of the day and night I have to shuffle, Mrs Overall-style, down the fields to break the ice on the water for the horses, lambs and chickens (someone told me that if I rub Vaseline on the chickens' cones, it keeps them warm. I spent days chasing them, trying to rub gloop on their beaks, only to find out later the person meant on their 'combs', not their little triangular mouths). I'm forever frantically pouring peanuts into the numerous birdfeeders I have dotted round the garden. The blue tits have become so naughty, so demanding, they actually tap on the window when they spy me huddling in my office, demanding Tilda basmati rice, served warm.

While I love my animals, I do feel like a maid in an upmarket animal spa, run ragged by their whims. Michael is the only one who seems remotely grateful. I've also taken a few steps backwards with Lizzie. We'd been progressing with our hacks rather well, going out for hours and hours on bridle paths through woods that looked as though they had been decorated by Swarovksi, but then, yesterday, I thought I'd ride her down to the village. We were pottering along, she was blinking her Penélope Cruz-lashed eyes in the dazzling sunlight, taking in the view, when suddenly she stopped dead, refusing to budge. She started flapping her lips, the first sign she is anxious, a sign you ignore at your peril in case she takes her stress to the next level. She might bite, or buck, or rear, or run backwards. That day, though, I'd run out of patience. I'd stopped listening to her.

'Come on, Lizzie,' I said crossly, totally fed-up that, after a year of nurturing her, she was being so stubborn. After all, we'd walked this lane in hand so many times. I dismounted, and as I turned her round, yanking her delicate, fine head roughly, I noticed a slick of black ice across the steep tarmac. She had seen the ice, somehow, and was worried she might slip, taking me down with her. She had been trying to look after me. 'I'm sorry, Lizzie,' I said, burying my face in her mane as we walked back up the hill towards home. 'I'm so, so sorry.' Sometimes, it seems, we are more loved, and less alone, than we know.

*

It's Christmas Day. I've put up a tree in my sitting room and garlanded it with lights and baubles. Michael momentarily lost his head, thought he was still outside, and weed on it. He immediately realised his mistake, and if he could've done, he would have put his paw to his mouth. If he thinks you're about to tell him off, he still cowers.

Nic had come early for our inaugural Christmas Day ride; we'd saddled up and set off. We were gone for about an hour, and for the first time I rode Lizzie up my hill instead of getting off to save her back. She didn't mind. She was really proud of herself, in fact. I don't know if you have ever seen a horse look pleased, but this is exactly the expression on her face. I remembered not to take her saddle off straight away when we got back; it causes something bad, I don't remember quite what. I'd bought her a diamante browband for Christmas, which she looked very beautiful in. She has more nice things than I do now – I had to borrow some cotton wool pads from her grooming box the other day. But I don't mind one bit. She deserves to be spoilt. She has such big, beautiful, soft eyes, even despite the tiny white spec of a scar, the only evidence she'd ever had a thorn in there. For lunch I've invited Nic and her dog Zac, Kevin and Nic's mum. We're having nut roast made with hazelnuts and chestnuts I found myself in the wood. Michael had soon got the hang of it and would bring me nuts in his mouth; sometimes they were just stones, but I didn't like to discourage him. We're also having baked potatoes (Brian – Brain –

had taught me that when the potatoes' leaves die off, it means the spuds are ready), tiny Brussel sprouts like bullets, teeny tiny parsnips, and leeks as slender as pencils, all dug from the dark, wet earth: it's like a feast for a doll. But not too bad for my first year's produce. Next year, I want to be self-sufficient in hay, carrots, apples, herbs, eggs and all the vegetables I can eat, including exotic things like asparagus. There is, I've found, nothing, not even something eaten in one of Gordon Ramsay's establishments, that tastes quite like a home-grown potato baked slowly in the Aga. Every time I make a cross in the top of a fluffy King Edward and breathe in its warm aroma, I feel quite like Milly Molly Mandy, who lived in her little village and whose greatest joy was a potato baked in a bonfire.

For Christmas Day pudding we're having apple crumble made with my own apples from an orchard that suddenly seemed to rally, or at least have had IVF, and produced glorious bright green cookers, although I forgot the crumble part. I realise, as we all sit around the big table with the brass cup handles on the drawers, that if someone were to peek in my window, they might just think I'm happy, normal (well, relatively), and loved.

CHAPTER 28

* * *

(In which I realise I won't end up in a scratchy tweed skirt, all the veins having burst on my face, millionaire potential boyfriend or no millionaire potential boyfriend, ex-husband or no ex-husband, rock star or no rock star)

It's New Year's Eve. I wake up early, extract myself from under the sleeping forms of Susie, Squeaky and Sweetie (they're all in the shape of commas) and go downstairs to grind some of Emily's espresso beans and make myself a perfect pot of coffee. Michael, 'my new boyfriend', the best boyfriend a girl could have, who's been sleeping on the Jasper Morrison sofa next to the Aga, which still isn't pistachio but will do, stretches his neck heavenwards as if he's about to howl, then pushes his warm, pointy nose into my hand. His brown eyes are filled with love.

I shuffle to the back porch in my cashmere socks and oversize men's pyjamas, unlock the huge church-like door and sit on the freezing flagstones. It was minus nine degrees last night; it's barely above freezing this morning. I hug the mug to keep me warm. It's a winter wonderland, with mist trapped in the valleys. The moon has forgotten to go home. I don't think I've ever seen a sight more breathtaking: not the Himalayas, not the Alps, not the private beach at Ian Fleming's house on Jamaica. Lizzie must've heard the beans grinding because she's walking up the hill towards me, her breath making little clouds. She has icicles in her mane. The lambs – they will always be the lambs, never the ewes, much as I will always be a girl rather than a woman – call to me impatiently; I'm so glad they have their thick jumpers, far more beautiful than anything by Dolce & Gabbana. Sweetie joins me, winding at my feet, doing her little bark, trying to tell me all about her latest mischief.

Later, I call Lizzie in and, entourage intact – Lizzie does love her entourage: Quincy, Benji, Dream and now poor, damaged Maggie – she walks into the yard. She stands stock still as I take off her warm rug – the Prada of rugs – peel off her aerobics vest, tack her up and put her boots on, pumping her up like a bicycle, a fleece over her ample rump to keep off the chill, not even bothering to tie her up. She occasionally turns her head to nibble my hair and search my pockets. I get on her gently from my padded mounting block and with Michael (also in a matching warm fleece) all proud at her heels, the end of her tail held gently in his mouth, we walk out of my gate onto the lane, the reins a loose loop on her short, muscled neck. I see several pairs of horse ears over the hedge, semaphoring to her.

It's quiet, apart from the hee-hee of a kestrel circling overhead; with no iron shoes, Lizzie doesn't sound like a horse, more like a camel: pad, pad, pad. Lizzie looks around her, taking in the icicles on the trees, the oak leaves on the ground that have been coated in frosting, as if placed there by Martha Stewart just for our benefit. Lizzie is eager, eating up the lane with her stride. We head down a hill, then turn left onto a bridle path. We cross over a stream, wind between gorse bushes, occasionally surprising a sheep, upsetting a rabbit, until we hit open moorland, the grass so closely cropped it's like velvet or moss; perhaps it is moss. I still don't know all the different names of things. We see a herd of Exmoor ponies in the distance. Lizzie wickers to them and they lift their heads, blowing steam.

My phone vibrates. I take it out of my pocket and reluctantly peel off one glove to click on a message. It's from the Millionaire. 'I hope you have a wonderful New Year, wherever you are. From one animal lover to another. I look forward to seeing you soon for dinner! X' I don't click reply. I put the phone back in my pocket. It goes off again, doing its merry shuffle in my pocket. 'Sorry, Lizzie,' I say, rubbing her sweet spot, and she twirls her huge ears. It's a text from my ex-husband. 'Can we meet for dinner on Tuesday? How about the veggie place on New North Road? It's nothing fancy, but it's within my budget.' Reader, I am not going to remarry him. I snap the phone shut and we turn towards the west.

Somehow, and I think Lizzie has something to do with this, we head alongside the river for a bit towards the middle of the moor, towards Simonsbath. We head down a hill, through a wood, alongside a cattle grid, and come to a great big pair of crumbling pillars, seemingly leading nowhere. Michael wees on a discreet sign, then stands and wags expectantly. 'Xxxx Manor House.' Ah. So this is where he's been hiding. 'Betcha By Golly Wow' (the Prince version) pops into my head. I hum it to Michael. 'You're the one that I've been waiting for for-e-ver.' I lean down onto the neck of my horse, breathing in her horse scent, so delicious someone should bottle it. 'I love you, I love you, I love you,' I tell her. There is nothing like being on a warm horse on a cold day.

USEFUL NAMES, NUMBERS
AND WEBSITES

* * *

If you're thinking about taking on a former racehorse, visit both of the websites below and have a good read first. Thoroughbred horses are ruinously expensive to look after and can be highly strung and difficult (like me, etc, etc). But the people who run these charities are knowledgeable and not scary or too horsey at all.

www.racehorsesgreatwood.org is based in Marlborough, Wiltshire, and as well as rescuing and rehoming racehorses uses equines to help children with special needs. Greatwood holds open days when you can go along, see the horses and talk to members of staff. If you're still keen, they will require references (both financial and horsey), and will conduct a home visit. Racehorses are only sent out on loan, never sold. Examples of horses this charity has helped in recent years include:
- a horse abandoned in a field having been 'won' in a pub over a game of cards
- a horse left in a scrapyard, the remains of his rug had

to be cut from him, his leg had been broken at some stage and had been left unnoticed
- a horse left alone in the dark to starve in its stable
- a horse dumped at a livery yard, and no one stepped forward to help him, let alone give him a morsel of feed
- a horse advertised free on the internet; its feet were so bad that he couldn't take a step without agony.

www.heroscharity.org is based in Oxfordshire and has rehomed over 300 racehorses. Like Greatwood, it requires references and a home visit before you will be allowed to take on a racehorse.

A fantastic lobbying body is Animal Aid. As well as campaigning against factory farming and blood sports, it does a forensic job monitoring the racing industry. Visit **www.animalaid.org.uk**

www.projecthorses.co.uk I found Lizzie on Project Horses, where you can view a directory of horses and ponies to buy or that are being offered on loan. The horses and ponies do generally have problems, but these should be made clear by the owner. Do, though, get the animal vetted and insured before you accept liability; this simple precaution will avoid you taking on an animal with unexpected problems you might not be able to treat. If you do rescue a horse or pony, ensure you have the passport from the owner before you take possession, and do have a letter signed by the owner saying that they have handed over ownership to you. You don't want to spend ages getting a horse or pony right, only for the original owner to ask for it back. Do inform the passport issuer of the change of ownership.

Many horses and ponies on this site are advertised as companions only. People, including me, tend to think of ponies as companions, but generally, horses and ponies have very different needs. Do consider an older horse as a companion, not just a cute pony (ponies tend to be naughtier than horses and harder to look after). If you do need a companion, another really good site is the Trallwm Farm Animal Sanctuary in Wales: it does great work. **www.trallwmfarm.org.uk**

If you love horses and just want to help, or alert someone to a horse that you think is being abused or neglected, contact **www.equinemarketwatch.org.uk**. I'm proud to say I'm now the patron of this wonderful horse, donkey and pony rescue charity that monitors horse and pony sales in the UK.

Or contact another organisation, World Horse Welfare, the new name for the International League for the Protection of Horses. **www.worldhorsewelfare.org**

The Brooke does wonderful work in developing countries, in some of the world's poorest and toughest environments, from Guatemala to Himalayan north-west Pakistan, helping the local people to look after their working animals and in turn to help themselves. **www.thebrooke.org**

Exmoor ponies

If you ever find yourself on Exmoor, do visit the Exmoor Pony Centre just outside Dulverton, which does great work rehabilitating ponies, handling foals to prepare them for rehoming, and conserving this rare and very special breed. It's a great way for children to get close to these amazing animals. **www.themoorlandmousietrust.org.uk**

Equine behaviourist

Nicola Bebb: **www.holisticequine.co.uk**

Nicola is a specialist in equine health, management and training. Founded by Nicola, Holistic Equine is the culmination of many years' love of horses and a desire to learn as much as possible to improve their welfare. Holistic Equine aims to bring you the best in a union of classic, contemporary and alternative equine care and understanding. Of all the people I have met in the horse world, Nicola is the most knowledgeable and the most patient. She really loves the horses she works with and will never cut corners. Lizzie kept presenting us with so many problems that it was hard to know what to tackle first, but Nicola was calm and methodical, oozing skill, expertise and love at all times.

Saddler

Lavinia Mitchell makes her own saddles. There are good, horse-friendly design features, on wider trees, all leather and English-made. Comfortable for the riders too! Just simple 'back to basic' no frills, good-quality saddles. **www.laviniamitchell.com**

Barefoot trimmer

Debbie Survila is knowledgeable and really thorough. She takes her time, never rushes the horses and is gentle. She'll also give you advice on how to care for your horse's feet between visits, and will show you how to use a weigh tape, which is essential if you have a pony that is prone to laminitis. She also trims lambs' hooves. **Debbie@balancedreason.co.uk**

A good website to read up on barefoot trimming first is **www.equinepodiatry.net**

McTimoney chiropractor

This is a very gentle, non-invasive form of chiropractice, especially good for animals that are in pain and nervous. Lindy Mitchell is based in Withypool, Somerset. Telephone: 01643 831478. Lindy is very knowledgeable, helpful and also treats humans.

Nutritionist

The wonderful Roger at Trinity Consultants will give advice on behavioural and physical problems, and prescribe food and supplements accordingly. Operates a very efficient mail-order service. Visit **www.justbespoke.com**

Kinesiologist and all-round psychic healer

Terry Shubrook: email **Terry.shu@sky.com**
Terry helped me get Snoopy back from the brink, and he'll
work with any animal, from a dog with fear aggression to
a horse with laminitis. He will travel within reason, but
can also do consultations over the telephone.

Feed

A really good website to read up fully on how to feed and
manage your horse is that operated by Simple System, a
great company that gives advice on bedding and feed,
which you can then buy online. All feed is molasses- and
additive-free. These are also ethical feeds in a world where
too many people do not have enough to eat. Forages,
especially lucerne, and linseed, grow well in poor soils and
use low levels of inputs.

Lucerne reduces soil compaction due to its deep roots,
and since it fixes nitrogen it releases this slowly into the
soil, reducing the need for nitrogen applications in sub-
sequent cereal crops; lucerne itself never needs nitrogen
applications. Lucerne remains in the ground for three to
four years, eliminating the need for annual cultivations,
which is very carbon-friendly. Linseed, also a low-input
crop, is also a fantastic feed for horses. And, of course,
forages are the natural feed of horses, not humans.
www.simplesystem.co.uk

Grazing

This is not as simple as just sticking a horse in a field to eat grass, oh dear me no. Sheep do, in fact, eat all the long bits of grass – the living hay – leaving behind the short, sugary stuff that make ponies fatter. Horses are predators: they prey on plants. Leave the grass long, and they will move around more, seeking out tasty morsels. Horses need the long, fibrous stuff for two reasons. Firstly, it is what they need and want to extract energy, they are fibre digesters, not sugar digesters. Secondly, they are eating living hay and as such once their gut and stomach are stretched, they stop eating. Unlike us they cannot overrule this fact of nature because they need to lift their heads to help the digestion process. Horses with their heads down all the time risk a number of digestion-related conditions.

For advice on land management, email a fantastically helpful man called Garry Holter, who will advise on how to avoid mud, laminitis and spending huge amounts on unnecessary supplements. Email him on **dgmholter@btinternet.com**

Worms

Overzealous worming can give ponies dangerous laminitis, so I think it's best to send off samples of the animal's dung for a worm count: you will be introducing far fewer chemicals into your horse's gut and, ultimately, it will be safer and cheaper to only worm when necessary. Intelligent Worming is the modern equivalent to traditional worming. The company will write a worming programme for your horse or pony, you then mail them the dung samples, which they then examine in a lab. If worms are present, they will post out the wormer to you. **www.intelligentworming.co.uk**

Sheep

These creatures are so intelligent and inquisitive, they make fantastic pets. Visit **www.shetland-sheep.org.uk** for advice on how to care for them. Shetlands have the highest quality wool of any native breed: it's very fine, soft and hard-wearing. The breed is very hardy, and the lambs have a terrific will to live and are very lively, playful and cheerful (unlike me, etc, etc). Contrary to popular opinion, Shetlands (all sheep, in fact) appreciate and will use a dry, draught-proof shelter. Hay should be fed if the grass is poor or frozen, but in winter do also feed organic lamb or ewe nuts and provide a special sheep lick for nutrients and, of course, fresh water. Don't allow sheep to eat horse feed as the copper can kill them, and do not overfeed. A good website for general advice is **www.bar-kingrock.com**. Sheep, if not destined to be eaten, are generally slaughtered at a few years of age when the fleece is considered not as good quality, and they can no longer have as many lambs. However, a sheep can live into its twenties if cared for properly.

Chickens

If you want to adopt a former battery hen or need advice on how to care for yours, visit **www.bhwt.org.uk** or **www.downthelane.net**

At first I made the mistake of housing my chickens overnight in a big stone barn, not realising it would be too cold for them and that rats could get in. A wooden, smallish chicken house is best, so that they can snuggle close together when it gets cold; you can then let them out each morning.

If you want to adopt a dog, visit **www.freewebs.com/ manytearsrescue.** This family-run charity rehomes pedigree dogs that were once used for breeding, or puppies not 'perfect' enough to make the grade.

If you fancy a Border collie, contact:

Border Collie Trust (GB) B.C.T. Rescue Centre, Heath Way, Narrow Lane, Colton, Nr Rugeley, Staffs WS15 3LY. Telephone: 01889 577058. Email: **bctgb@bordercollietrustgb.org.uk**.

Don't be put off by the collie websites that say these former working dogs are difficult and find it hard to adapt to life as a pet. They do need lots of exercise and want to be with you for most of the day, but they're so intelligent and loving, they really are worth the time and effort. Michael and I are now engaged.

Further reading

The Chosen Road by K.C. La Pierre (purchase at **www.aepsupplies.co.uk**)

Equine Behaviour: A Guide for Veterinarians and Equine Scientists by Paul McGreevy (Saunders)

Improve Your Horse's Well-Being by Linda Tellington-Jones (Kenilworth Press)

A Good Horse is Never a Bad Colour and *Horses Never Lie: The Art of Passive Leadership* by Mark Rashid (David & Charles)

Riding between the Worlds by Linda Kohanov (New World Library). This book is quite way out, but I like that she treats her herd of horses as equals, which of course they are. Her philosophy is that horses are not to be owned by us for reasons of ego or pleasure. They shouldn't be owned at all, merely helped and looked after, as they help and look after us.

The Classical Seat, Invisible Riding and *Dressage in Lightness* by Sylvia Loch (A Horse's Mouth Publication); also visit **www.classicalriding.co.uk**

ACKNOWLEDGEMENTS

* * *

My thanks to Robert Caskie, Alan Samson, Lucinda McNeile, Rebecca Gray, Clare Wallis, Bee Murphy, Helen Ewing, Sue Peart, Nicola Bebb and, of course, all the animals.